SEMIOTEXT(E) INTERVENTION SERIES

© Maurizio Lazzarato, 2021. Originally published in French by Éditions Amsterdam.

Published by Semiotext(e)
PO BOX 629, South Pasadena, CA 91031
www.semiotexte.com

Design: Hedi El Kholti

ISBN: 978-1-63590-138-2
Distributed by the MIT Press, Cambridge, Mass.,
and London, England
Printed in the United States of America
10 9 8 7 6 5 4 3 2

Maurizio Lazzarato

Capital Hates Everyone

Fascism or Revolution

Translated by Robert Hurley

semiotext(e)
intervention
series □ 29

Contents

Introduction: Apocalyptic Times   7

1. When Capital Goes to War   19

2. Technical Machine and War Machine   118

3. Becoming-Revolutionary and Revolution   207

Notes   237

Introduction

Apocalyptic Times

"Without thought going to the limit, no strategy, thus no tactic, thus no action, thus no real thinking or initiative, thus no writing, no music, no painting, no sculpture, etc., are possible."
— Louis Althusser

We are living in "apocalyptic" times, in the literal sense of the word—times that manifest, times that reveal. What they show, firstly, is that the financial collapse of 2008 initiated a period of political ruptures. The alternative "fascism or revolution" is asymmetrical, out of balance, because we are already inside a seemingly irresistible series of "political ruptures" created by neo-fascist, sexist, racist forces; because for the moment, the revolutionary rupture is just a hypothesis, dictated by the necessity of reintroducing what neoliberalism has succeeded in erasing from the memory, the action, and the theory of the forces combating capitalism. This is even its most important victory.

What these apocalyptic times also show is that the new fascism is the other face of neoliberalism. Wendy Brown confidently asserts a contrary truth: "From the viewpoint of the first neoliberals, the galaxy that includes Trump, Brexit, Orbán, the Nazis, or the German Parliament, the fascists in the Italian Parliament, is turning the neoliberal dream into a nightmare. Hayek, the ordoliberals, or even the Chicago school would repudiate the current form of neoliberalism and especially its most recent guise."[1] This is not only false from a factual standpoint, it is also problematic for understanding capital and the exercise of its power. By erasing the "violence that founded" neoliberalism, incarnated by the bloody dictatorships of South America, one commits a double, political and theoretical, error: one concentrates only on the "violence that preserves" the economy, the institutions, law, and governmentality—tested out for the first time in Pinochet's Chile—and so one presents capital as an agent of modernization, as a power of innovation; moreover, one erases the world revolution and its defeat, which however are the origin and cause of "globalization" as the global response of capital.

The conception of power that results from this is pacified: action upon action, government upon behaviors (Foucault) and not action upon persons (of which war and civil war are the peak expressions).

Power would be incorporated into impersonal apparatuses that exert a soft violence in an automatic way. Quite to the contrary, however, the logic of civil war that is at the foundation of neoliberalism was not absorbed, erased, replaced by the functioning of the economy, law, and democracy.

The apocalyptic times show us that the new fascisms are in the process of reactivating—although no communism is threatening capitalism and property—the relationship between war and "governmentality." We are living in a period of blurring, of hybridization of the State of law and the state of exception. The hegemony of neofascism must not be measured simply by the strength of its organizations, but also by the capacity it has to bleed into the State and the political and media system.

The apocalyptic times reveal that beneath the democratic façade, behind the economic, social, and institutional "innovations," one always finds the class hatred and violence of strategic confrontation. It only took a movement of rupture like the Yellow Vests, who have nothing revolutionary, or even pre-revolutionary, about them, for the "spirit of Versailles" to awaken, for a new upwelling of the desire to shoot those "pieces of shit" who were not threatening, even symbolically, power and property. When there is an interruption of the time of capital, even a bourgeois editorialist can grasp a bit of emergent reality: "The current empire of hate is resuscitating boundaries of class and caste, sometimes long dormant [...]. One is seeing that acid of hate which eats away at democracy and suddenly submerges a decomposed, destructured, unstable, fragile, unpredictable political society—the ancient hatred resurfacing in the faltering France of the 21st century. Underneath modernity, hatred."[2]

The apocalyptic times also manifest the strength and weaknesses of the political movements which, since 2011, have tried to contest the supreme power of capital. This book was completed during the Yellow Vests uprising. Adopting the viewpoint of "world revolution" in order to read such a movement (but also the different Arab Springs, Occupy Wall Street in the U.S., the M15 in Spain, the days of June 2013 in Brazil, etc.) might seem pretentious or fantastical. And yet "thinking at the limit" means starting again not only from the historical defeat suffered in the 1960s by world revolution, but also from the "unrealized possibilities" which were created by and included revolutions, differently in the North and in the South, and which are still timidly mobilized in contemporary movements.

The form of the revolutionary process had already changed in the 1960s, but it had come up against an insurmountable obstacle: the inability to invent a different model from the one that, in 1917, had begun the long string of 20th century revolutions. In the Leninist model, revolution still had the form of *realization*. The working class was the subject that already contained the conditions of the abolition of capitalism and the installation of communism. The passage from "class in itself" to "class for itself" needed to be *realized* through the *prise de conscience* and the seizure of power, organized and led by the party that brought in from the outside what was lacking in the "trade-union" practices of the workers.

Since the 1960s, however, the revolutionary process has taken the form of the event: political subjects, instead of being already there in the making, are "unforeseen" (the Yellow Vests are a paradigmatic example of this unforeseeability); they don't embody history's necessity, but only the contingency of political confrontation. Their constitution, their "coming-to-consciousness," their program, their organization are formed on the basis of a refusal (to be governed), a rupture, a radical *here and now* that aren't satisfied with any promise of democracy and justice to come.

To be sure, with all due respect to Rancière, the uprising has its "reasons" and its "causes." The Yellow Vests are more intelligent than the philosopher, because they have "understood" that the relationship between "production" and "circulation" has been reversed. Circulation, the circulation of money, commodities, human beings, and information now takes precedence over "production." They no longer occupy the factories, but the roundabouts, and attack the circulation of information (the circulation of currency being more abstract, targeting it requires another level of organization and action).

The precondition for the emergence of the political process is obviously a rupture with the "reasons" and "causes" that generated it. Only the interruption of the existing order, only the exit from governmentality will be able to open up a new political process, because the "governed," even when they resist, are power's double, its correlates, its opposite numbers. Rupture with the time of domination, by creating new possibilities, unimaginable before their appearance, establishes the conditions for the transformation of self and the world. But no mystique of the riot, no idealism of the uprising is called for.

The processes of constitution of the political subject, the forms of organization, the development of capabilities for the struggle, made possible by an interruption of the time of power, are immediately confronted with the "reasons" of profit, property, and patrimony which the uprising has not caused to disappear. On the contrary, they are more aggressive, they immediately invoke the re-establishment of order, placing the police at the forefront, while continuing, as if nothing had happened, the promulgation of "reforms." Here the alternatives are radical: either the new political process manages to change capital's "reasons," or those same reasons will change it. The opening up of political possibilities is confronted with the reality of a formidable double problem, that of the constitution of a political subject and that of the power of capital, because the former can only take place within the latter.

The responses given to these questions by the Arab Springs, Occupy Wall Street, the days of June 2013 in Brazil, etc., are very weak; the movements continue to experiment without finding real strategies. These impasses cannot in any way be overcome by the "left populism" practiced by Podemos in Spain. Its strategy realizes the liquidation of the revolution begun in the aftermath of '68 by many Marxists whose Marxism had failed. Democracy as the locus of conflicts and subjectification replaces capitalism-and-revolution (Lefort, Laclau, Rancière), at the very moment when capital's machine is literally swallowing up "democratic representation." Claude Lefort's assertion, "in democracy, the place of power is empty" is contradicted as early as the start of the 1970s: that place is occupied by the *sui generis* "sovereign" that capital is. Every party that installs itself there can only function as its "authorized signatory" (many have scoffed at the Marxian simplification, but it has been completely realized, caricaturally so, by the latest president of the French Republic, Emmanuel Macron). Left populism gives new life to something that no longer exists. Representation and the Parliament hold no power, the latter being entirely concentrated in the executive, which, in neoliberalism, executes not the orders of the "people" or the general interest, but those of capital and property.

The desire to politicize the movements of post-2008 reveals itself to be reactionary, since it imposes precisely what the revolution of the 1960s had rejected and what is rejected by every movement that has emerged since: the (charismatic) leader, the "transcendence" of the party, the delegation of representation, liberal democracy, the people. The positioning of left populism (and its theoretical systematization by Laclau and Mouffe) prevents one from naming the enemy. Its categories ("caste," "those from above" and "those from below") are one step from conspiracy theory and two steps from its culmination, the denunciation of "international Jewry" that would be controlling the world via finance. These confusions, carefully maintained by the leaders and theorists of an impossible populism of the left, continue to plague the movements. In the case of the Yellow Vests, they are maintained by the media and the political system while expressing the vagueness that still characterizes the modalities of the rupture. It must be said that in the contemporary political desert, battered by fifty years of counter-revolution, getting one's bearings is not an easy matter.

The limits of the Yellow Vests movement, those of all the movements that have deployed since 2011 are evident, but no "external' force, no party can claim the prerogative, as the Bolsheviks had done, of showing "what is to be done" and how to do it. These indications can only come from the interior, in an immanent way. Here the interior is constituted, among other things, by the knowledge, the experience, the viewpoints of other political movements, because the struggles of the Yellow Vests, unlike the "working class," aren't capable of representing the whole proletariat, nor of expressing the critique of all the dominations that constitute capitalism's machine.

The movement of the "colonized from within," constituted in terms of the North/South division, which reproduces a "third world" in countries of the center, necessarily implies, at the same time as the critique of internal segregation, the critique of the international domination of capital, of the global exploitation of labor power and the resources of the planet—which are singularly lacking in the Yellow Vests. Without this "racial" and international component of capitalism, the movement sometimes projects the image of a France-centric nationalism. But no illusion about the national space is possible: the nation-state, in the 19th century, owed its existence to the global dimension of colonialist capitalism and the welfare state owed its existence to world revolution and the planetary strategic confrontation of the Cold War.

The racial fracture of which the "colonized" were the victims divided not only the global organization of labor, but even the revolution of the 1960s. Today, the conditions of possibility of a world revolution reside, on the one hand, in the invention of a new internationalism, which the movements of neo-colonized people (migrants, first of all) embody almost physically and which the movements of women are currently the only ones to mobilize thanks to their worldwide networks; and, on the other hand, in the critique of capitalist hierarchies, which musn't be limited to the sphere of labor. The sexual and racial divisions structure not only the reproduction of capital but also the distribution of social functions and roles.

Today, a movement focused on the "social question" cannot be spontaneously socialist as in the 19th and 20th centuries, because the global and social revolution (involving all power relations) has gone beyond that. Without a critique of the racial and social divisions, the movement exposes itself to all the possible recuperations (on the part of the right and the extreme right), which it has been able, in spite of everything, to resist until now. If the subjectivities that carry the struggles against these different dominations cannot be reduced to the unity of the "empty signifier" of the people, as left populism would have it, the double problem of common political action and the power of capital remains in its entirety. The inability to analyze the latter as both a *global* and a *social* machine, whose exploitation and domination don't end with "labor," is one of the fundamental causes of the defeat incurred in the 1960s. From this point of view, the strategy hasn't changed, we are far from having one.

Since 2011, the movements are "revolutionary" as to the forms of mobilization (inventiveness in the choice of the space and time of confrontation, radical democracy and great flexibility in the modes of organization, refusal of representation and of leaders, avoidance of centralization and totalization by a party, etc.) and "reformist" as to demands and definition of the enemy (Mubarak was ousted, but his system of power was left in place, similar to the way in which people concentrate their critique on Macron although he is simply, without any possible doubt, one component of capital's machine). And if the rupture leads to notable changes this is not in the organization of power and property, but in the subjectivity of the insurgents. And if in the short term the movements are defeated, the subjective changes will very likely continue to produce their political effects. Provided that one doesn't fall into the illusion that a "social revolution" can take place without a "political revolution"—that is, without going beyond capitalism.[3] Post-'68 demonstrated that when social revolution splits off from political revolution, it can easily be integrated into the capitalist machine as a new resource for the accumulation of capital. The "becoming-revolutionary" which these subjective conversions inaugurate cannot be separated from "revolution" if they don't want to become a component of capital, hence of its power of destruction and self-destruction, which is manifested today with neo-fascism.

1

When Capital Goes to War

> "The power of a dominant class doesn't result simply from its economic and political strength, or from the distribution of property, or from the transformation of the productive system; it always implies a historical triumph in the combat against the subaltern classes."
>
> — Michael Löwy

From Pinochet to Bolsonaro and Back

The election of Bolsonaro to the presidency of Brazil marks a radicalization of the neo-fascist, racist, and sexist wave that is sweeping the planet. It has the sole merit of elucidating, one hopes definitively, the political meaning of that wave. Calling it "populist" or "neoliberal-authoritarian" is a way of burying one's head in the sand.

If Bolsonaro's victory is shocking, this is because it traces back directly to the political birth of neo-liberalism, in the Chile of Pinochet. The government of Brazil, with generals in key posts and a neoliberal Minister of Economy and Finance, a student of the "Chicago Boys," is a mutation of the neoliberal experimentation built on the corpses of thousands of communist and socialists in Chile and all of Latin America. Milton Friedman, leader of the Chicago Boys, met with Pinochet in 1975; Hayek, the champion of "freedom," was received in Chile in 1977. He declared that "dictatorship may be necessary" and that "personal freedom is greater under Pinochet than under Allende." In "periods of transition," when, from what one can gather from his statements, one has the right to massacre those who don't submit to the freedom of the market, it is "inevitable that someone has absolute powers in order to avoid and limit all absolute power in the future." On that basis, for a decade (1975–1986), the neoliberal economists enjoyed "ideal" conditions for trying out their recipes, the bloody crushing of revolution having quashed all conflictuality, all opposition, all criticism.

Other countries of Latin America followed those "innovative" policies. Chicago Boys occupied key posts in Uruguay, Brazil, and Argentina. With the power grab of Videla, responsible with the military junta for another, perhaps even more horrific killing spree, the neoliberals entered into the government of the military officers and tried to reproduce the Chilean policies of massive wage reductions, cuts in social expenditures, privatization of schools, health care, pensions, etc. These policies were immediately recognized and adopted by the World Bank under the name that has remained its own: "structural adjustments." They would then be applied in Africa, South Asia and would only arrive much later in the North.

How is one to think about these phenomena? The analytical tradition that dominates today, initiated by Michel Foucault, completely ignores the grim, dirty, violent genealogy of neoliberalism, where military torturers rub shoulders with the criminals of economic theory. The problem this poses is not moral (indignation with regard to the armed crushing of the revolutionary processes of Latin America) but primarily theoretical and political. Governmentality, entrepreneurship of oneself, competition, freedom, "rationality" of the market, etc., all these fine concepts that Foucault found in books and never measured against real political processes (an assumed methodological choice!), have a presupposition that is never made explicit, but on the contrary is carefully effaced: the subjectivity of the "governed" can be constructed only on the condition of a more or less bloody defeat, which changes its status from that of political adversary to that of "loser."

Latin America is a textbook case in the matter. Its struggles belong to the postwar cycle of world revolution against colonialism and imperialism, a cycle that deeply destabilized capitalism and its economy-world. They produced levels of organization and antagonism with the West that were incomparable in their scope and intensity. It would have been impossible to demand or even suggest that these revolutionary subjectivities engaged in an overcoming of capitalism and its dominations think of themselves as "human capital," that they involve themselves in the competition of all against all, that they cultivate their selfishness and lust after individual "advancement" and "success." Never would that subjectivity have been made to believe that if it accepted the market, the state, the corporation, and individualism, it would have a "grip on its own life"; never would it have been possible to control it and lead it individually to "self-realization."

After Allende had won the elections and taken power through a democratic vote, the Americans decided to destroy this process militarily and physically eliminate the revolutionaries who were leading it. It was upon this subjective "tabula rasa," at the cost of thousands of deaths, that the neoliberal experiments were able to implant themselves, that the "defeated" were made "available" for an impossible "becoming-entrepreneurs" of themselves.

Neoliberalism doesn't believe, like its ancestor, in the "natural" functioning of the market; it knows it is necessary, on the contrary, to constantly intervene, to support it with juridical managers, fiscal incentives, economic incentives, etc. But there is a preliminary "interventionism" that is called "civil war," the only thing capable of creating the conditions for "disciplining" the "governed" having the presumptuousness to want revolution and communism. This is why the Chicago Boys descended like so many vultures on Latin America. In that part of the world there was a subjectivity devastated by military repression, whose political project had been defeated, and on which one could "freely" operate. This history, rapidly disappeared from the memory of political theory, is not a peculiarity of neoliberalism: before it, ordoliberalism was able to deploy its recipes only on German subjectivities wiped out by the Nazi experience.

In the postwar West, the revolutionary struggle never attained the intensity and scale it achieved in Latin America and the "global South" (from Vietnam to Algeria, from Cuba to the Congo, from Yemen to Angola and Mozambique, etc.). The organizations of the workers' movement were completely integrated into Keynesian governmentality and the new political subjects appearing during the Cold War proved incapable of thinking and organizing a process of rupture with capitalism, so that the defeat occurred in a different way. More than in the South, the "impossible revolution of

'68" was both anti-capitalist and anti-socialist. It sharply contested the political action that had been codified by the Russian and Chinese revolutions, but also the strategies of social democracy and the communist parties. Caught between a revolutionary model that was still basically that of the 19th century and a revolution for the 21st century which it was not able to invent, it ended in a historical defeat without any truly strategic confrontations. Despite the scale of the conflicts (millions of strikers in the factories, rebellions in the schools, revolt in the families and the psychiatric hospitals, insubordination in the army, etc.) the capitalists of the state were not confronted with true revolutions. It was enough for Thatcher to put down the miners and Reagan the air traffic controllers, for their "enemy" to collapse.

The rupture did not come from the multiplicity of movements of contestation (revolutionary attempts developed on the margin or in an isolated manner, such as in Italy where the repression was immediate and brutal) but from the corporations, the state, from conservative milieus which, as they noted they were not facing *political enemies*, but only *contestataires*, pushed their advantage ever further by formulating, over a ten year period, a veritable theory and practice of "counter-revolution." The methods were not the same as in the Chile of Pinochet, Friedman, and Hayek, but the modes of management of the powers exercised on the basis of diversely obtained victories and over diversely defeated "losers" rapidly converged.

The capitalists and their respective states always conceive their strategies (war, civil war, governmentality) in relation to the situation of the world market and the political dangers lurking there. They construct these strategies in response to the conflicts that unfold and adjust them according to the resistances, oppositions, and confrontations they encounter. But one shouldn't make the mistake of separating a "violent" South from a "pacified" North: it's the same capital, the same power, the same war. The neoliberals, guided by a class hatred lacking in their adversaries, made no mistake by mobilizing in Latin America. Not only because capitalism is immediately a "world market," but also because the revolution which, for the first time in history, revealed itself to be global, had its most active centers in the South. It had to be crushed as a preliminary to all "governmentality," even if this meant allying with—hence legitimating—fascists, torturers, and criminals. Something that liberals (neo- or not) are prepared to do and do again whenever "private property" is threatened, even potentially.

In the 20th century, capital confronted not only the conflictuality of labor, but also the greatest and most intense revolutionary cycle in history. The world revolution brought innovations that the revolutionaries were not able to recognize, valorize, and organize. Revolution doesn't depend on the development of the productive forces (labor, science, technology), but on the level of intensity of political organization; nor is it the exclusive pursuit of the working class, because, since the French Revolution, a large part of the victorious revolutions were carried out by "peasants."

To try and understand what is happening to us, one has to go back to the beginning of the 20th century. The Michael Löwy quote placed as an epigraph to this chapter is a faithful and effective synthesis of the thought of Walter Benjamin, one of the rare Marxists to have fully grasped the rupture represented by total wars and fascism. The definition he gives of capitalism broadens and radicalizes that of Marx, since for Benjamin capital is both production and war, power of creation and power of destruction: "only triumph over the subaltern classes" makes possible the transformations of the productive system, of law, of property, and of the state.

We find these dynamics at the foundation of neoliberalism, whose "historical triumph," in which fascism once again plays a central role, is focused on "world revolution." A victory over subaltern classes very different from those that Benjamin had in mind—like most European Marxists at the time, he had trouble appreciating the importance of the anti-colonial struggle. And yet, if Paris between the two wars was no longer, as in the 19th century, the capital of the epoch, it did play a determining role in the coming revolutions as "capital of the Third World." It was the training ground, at the junction of Asiatic, African, and South American migrations, for the great majority of the leaders who directed the national liberation against colonialism, the motor of world revolution.[1]

The total wars of the first half of the 20th century transformed war into industrial war and fascism into a mass organization of counter-revolution. We have behind us a century that allows us to claim that war and fascism are the *political* and *economic* forces necessary to capital's conversion of accumulation, something that was not evident in Marx's era. Without civil war and fascism, without "creative destruction," no conversion of the economic, juridical, state, and governmental apparatuses [*dispositifs*]. Since 2008, we have entered into a new sequence of this type.

Consequently, the difference between my analysis of neoliberalism and those of Foucault, of Luc Boltanski and Éve Chiapello or of Pierre Dardot and Christian Laval, is radical. Those authors erase the fascist origins of neoliberalism and the "world revolution" of the 1960s—which means limiting oneself to the French '68—but also the neoliberal counter-revolution, the ideological framework of capital's revenge. This difference has to do with the nature of capitalism which those theories "pacify" by erasing the political-military victory which is the precondition of its deployment. The "triumph" over the subaltern classes is part of the nature and the definition of capital, just like money, value, production, etc.

The Financialization of the Poor

The confrontation between political enemies of the 20th century ended with the victory of capital, which transformed the defeated into the "governed." Once the revolutionary alternatives were defeated and destroyed, once the subjective *tabula rasa* was carried out, new apparatuses were able to establish new norms for directing people and subjugating them.

A few days after the second round of the last presidential election, a Brazilian journalist, Eliane Brum, wrote: "when we begin to discuss an original project for the country, when the Indians, the Blacks, and the women begin to occupy new spaces of power, the process is interrupted, the war resumes. For in fact the war against the weakest has never stopped. It has slackened at times, but it has never stopped. This time, the perversion is that, so far, the authoritarian project has been installed with the trappings of democracy."[2]

Brum underscores a reality that everyone seems to repress: the war has never ceased. Its intensity is just modulated according to the conjunctures of the political confrontation. Within these "pacified" relations, the contradictions of the regime of financialized accumulation and the struggles conducted by the governed determine the conditions for new polarizations that, on the basis of the political sequence initiated by the breakdown of the financial system in 2008, will lead to the rupture of the governmentality established with Reagan and Thatcher.

In Brazil, we can follow this process step by step: from the end of the dictatorship to the putting in place of apparatuses of a financialized governance during the terms of Lula and Dilma Rousseff and, starting with the crisis of the latter, to new forms of strategic confrontation, crystallized by the election of Bolsonaro. What Brazil clearly shows is the *radical incompatibility of reformism with neoliberalism*, since the latter was conceived, constructed, intended precisely against the "Keynesian" experience. We'll analyze these different political sequences from a specific viewpoint, that of the "social policies" chosen by financial capital in order to impose its domination and which happen to be exactly the same as in the countries of the North.[3]

The Workers' Party (PT) had the plan of bringing about a "redistribution" of wealth based on "social expenditure"; it ended up financializing the latter, and in part, privatizing it. The transformation of poor people and a fraction of wage earners into "indebted men and women," which was consolidated and extended starting with Lula's first mandate, would have formidable consequences after the crisis of 2008. A confrontation between enemies was again on the agenda, but after forty years of neoliberalism, in very different circumstances: the rupture of governmentality was due to the use of democratic institutions by the extreme right and to the great weakness of the anti-capitalist movements, incapable of reorganizing and of defining a new strategy and new modes of revolutionary organization.

One of the pillars of the PT's "social developmentalism"—along with raising the minimum wage and wages in general, and the creation of the Bolsa Familia (a program of assistance to the poorest families)—was support for consumption. Consumption exploded thanks to the access to credit gained by the poor and the lower strata of wage earners (the other pillar of this developmentalism was constituted by the export of raw materials). During the last economic cycle, credit seems to have become nearly as important as wages for stimulating the growth of demand. If wages doubled, credit for consumption quadrupled—it accounted for more than 45% in the growth of family incomes and for a third in the growth of the GDP.

Access to credit, whose goal was to reduce poverty, also functioned as the Trojan horse by which financialization was introduced into the everyday life of millions of Brazilians, especially the poorest ("inclusion through finance"). The creditor/debtor relation is a technique making it possible to guide and control behaviors across the social groups, since it functions as well with the poor person as with the unemployed, the wage earner, the retiree. An extremely effective technique, which shifts the class struggle onto a new terrain, where workers' organizations have a hard time positioning themselves.[4]

The capture of new social groups (workers, poor people, and the working poor) in the circuit of debt was facilitated by the creation of the "*credito consignado*" by the PT's governing body: the banks would deduct the interest of the debt directly from the wages, retirement payments, and income transfers, thus insuring finance against the "risks." For the banks, this led to a lowering of costs enabling them to reduce the price of loans and thus broaden the circuit of financialization.

The PT succeeded in imposing one of the strategic objectives of neoliberalism: in the accumulation realized by finance, "the effective

Kaynesian demand" and the redistribution of wealth by the state should gradually be replaced by the privatization of state expenditures and social services (health care, education, unemployment compensation, retirement, etc). The financing of these expenditures would be ensured by a monetary creation reserved for the banks and financial institutions, which would multiply the techniques for facilitating the access to credit. In this way, the left-wing government furthered the realization of another, even more important, objective of the neoliberal agenda: the privatization of currency creation, from which all the other privatizations ensued. This strategy of commodification of social services constitutes both a machine for capturing wealth that still escapes the valorization of financial capital, a formidable apparatus of production of a *subjectivity for the market*, and an attempt at redefining the functions of the state.

With the increasing replacement of Keynesian "effective demand" and policies of redistribution by the privatization of services and currency, finance has taken control, in Brazil and elsewhere, of "social reproduction" and its financing. Neither the workers' movement, nor the feminist movement have been able to offer real alternatives to this appropriation/privatization of "reproduction" which the feminist currents calling for "wages for housework" have diagnosed as strategic since the 1970s.

Lena Lavinas has very accurately described the acquiescence of the PT leadership to the directives of the financial institutions of global governance, which, at least since 2000, advocate "inclusion through financialization" and stimulation of growth through credit for consumption, which they consider to be the most effective means of fighting poverty. After the financial meltdown of 2008, the World Bank, the IMF, and the G20 wanted to accelerate the development of "inclusive financial systems" to reduce inequalities and establish an "equality of opportunity." Capital's self-destructive madness—its suicidal core—carefully blotted out by a left that attribute to it a power of progress and modernization it has never had, reveals itself once again: resolve the crisis using the techniques that produced it.

But the neoliberal strategy is not "economic" without being subjective at the same time: "The economic sciences are the method, the goal is to change hearts and minds," said Margaret Thatcher. The new policies of social protection are a radical break from the principles of the postwar welfare state since they aim to "protect the basic means of subsistence while encouraging risk-taking" by the individual. They pressure the poor to transform their behavior so as to be capable of individually taking on the risks that indebtedness involves.

The "social risks" that had been assumed collectively, first by workers' risk-sharing, then by the welfare state, must now be taken on by the individual (welfare, though it's a means of controlling workers by nationalizing the modes of mutual solidarity, did preserve the principle of the socialization of risks). This covering over of social risks by the individual risk of indebtedness is conceived by the financial institutions as a technique of subjugation, the regular repayments imposing a discipline on the borrowers, a form of life, a way of thinking and acting. In the view of the World Bank, such a self-control is essential for transforming the poor individual into an entrepreneur who can manage the irregularity of his income flow thanks to credit.

These new techniques of governmentality, very different from the Fordist apparatuses of power, are designed to create the conditions (economic incentives, tax allowances, etc.) for orienting the "choices" of the individual towards the private sphere through a micropolitical social engineering that is basically financial: instead of providing services, one distributes money, or better still, credit which the individual will spend on the market of service providers that is open to competition. The social user thus transforms himself into an indebted customer.

The PT also carried out, unknowingly, another element of the neoliberal program that was quickly turned back against it: the reconfiguring of the state and its functions. Far from the neoliberal mind was the idea of a "weak state," a minimum state, or certainly a "phobia of the state." Quite the opposite, the privatization of services should free the state from the pressure that social struggles exerted on its expenditures. Instead of being the site of the exercise of sovereignty necessary to the unhindered development of private property, during the entire Cold War the political system was besieged by demands that sapped the authority of the state and stretched its administrative functions (this is the message of the Trilateral Commission's report of 1975).[5]

Privatizing the "offer" of services means taking away from "social demand" its political dimension and its collective form. Once rid of "expectations," the rights and the equality that the struggles bring along with them, it will be able to assume the functions that neoliberalism envisages for it: it will become "a strong state, for a free economy," "a state strong with the weak (the have-nots) and weak with the strong (the property-owners)." It must not become minimum, but organize and manage "minimum services"—that is, ensure a minimal coverage of risks, because the rest must be bought on the insurance market. Those who don't keep up with the pace of competition, those who fall outside the labor market, have available a "minimum" with which to start over and re-enter the competition of all against all (workfare). Moreover, it's the state itself which must work toward this transformation, by *underfinancing* the services, by *allowing* them to degrade and by putting in place fiscal policies that encourage the recourse to credit. This is in fact what the Brazilian state gradually implemented.

In Brazil, during Lula's terms in office, the consequences were miserable: indebtedness, individualization, and depoliticization, without the "growth" and the redistribution modifying the class structure, even marginally. Inclusion through finance didn't subvert the highly unequal social and productive structures; on the contrary, it reproduced them, because the distribution through credit only produced a "superficial consumerism." Lavinas remarks that "in only a decade, the ownership of durable goods such as cellphones, color televisions and refrigerators became almost universal," whatever the disposable income, while Perry Anderson underscores the limits of this consumerist strategy: "The water supply, paved roads, efficient buses, acceptable sewage disposal, decent schools and hospitals were neglected. Collective goods had neither ideological nor practical priority"[6] The great mobilizations of 2013, which developed outside the PT and against it, were the manifestation of frustration, anger, and disappointment concerning the results of these social policies. The demands were aimed precisely at the deterioration of public transportation, health services, and education. They sounded the death knell of the PT's "soft reformism."

The PT sawed off the limb on which it was sitting because its "redistribution" policies created a depoliticizing individualism that was actually the political goal sought by the neoliberals. According to Anderson, "[t]he poor remained passive beneficiaries of PT rule, which had never educated or organized them, let alone mobilized them as a collective force...Distribution there was, appreciably raising the living standards of the least well-off, but it was individualized in form." Lavinas added to this, giving a definition of the PT that one could synthesize by calling it *credit card socialism*. "Once in power, the Workers' Party reckoned that it was possible to refound the nation by creating new social identities, resting not on ties of collective belonging or communitarian solidarity, but rather on access to credit, a personal bank account or a credit card."

The illusion of a growth (or, more exactly, an accumulation of capital) which would only create winners and be capable of reconciling the classes by mobilizing them for the project of a grand Brazil, shattered on the consequences of the financial collapse of 2008 and the internal weaknesses of a redistribution project based on finance (but also on the lowering of the prices of the raw materials of "extractive" capitalism, which Bolsonaro would revive by amplifying the process of deforestation of Amazonia, which the PT itself favored).

Neoliberalism did not arrive at the end of Lula's presidency; the irony is that it was cultivated by the Workers' Party. Capital, it should be said, maintains excellent relations with the institutions of the workers' movement, since financialization would have been inconceivable without the "pension funds" of American wage earners (teachers, civil servants, workers, etc.), big institutional investors in the stock markets.

But as soon as there is a danger, albeit one created by capital itself, there is a rebuilding of alliances of international finance with fascism, agribusiness landholders, military leaders, and clergy (reactionary Catholics in the period of dictatorship, evangelicals today), in the very classic strategy which the neoliberals had no problem legitimating.

Aside from these movements of big capital, the rebellion and desire for vengeance of the white elites and upper-middle classes found the political space manifesting themselves. The class hatred provoked by a worker president, by the quotas guaranteeing the enrollment of Blacks in the universities or by the obligation to establish labor contracts for maids (strictly non-white) was expressed when the failure of the economic policies became evident. But it is quite possible that the sad affects of the indebted individual, both guilty and frustrated, fearful and isolated, worried and depoliticized, also made some of the poor and the wage earners susceptible to fascist adventures. The micropolitics of credit created the conditions for a fascist micropolitics.

Strategic confrontations returned to the agenda, therefore, after the folly of the neoliberal recipes had failed everywhere, and not only in Brazil. But this rupture of governmentality found the political movements completely unprepared as, since 1985, year of the end of the dictatorship, they have neglected to analyze the new conditions of war, of the civil war and revolution. Strategic thinking, which constituted an asset of the revolutionary movements in the 19th and 20th centuries, is what was completely missing from the planetary wave of mobilizations of 2011, in which the Brazilian movement of 2013 has its place.

The experience of Latin America during the period of neoliberalism was built on a big misunderstanding relative to "reformism." "Reformism" is not an alternative to revolution for it depends on the latter's reality or its threat (a possible revolution). Without the real endangerment of capitalism, no reformism. The political movements of the 19th century—socialist, anarchist, communist—all pursued the supersession or destruction of capitalism. Despite the bloody political "defeats" undergone throughout the century, the social conquests progressed. The Russian Revolution brought this cycle of struggles to its completion and, in spite of its political failure, it worked, with the cycle of anticolonial revolutions, towards the winning of new rights, including in the West (welfare, workers rights, etc.). The contemporary political movements are very far from threatening the existence of capital, so that, for forty years, the socio-economic defeats are equivalent to political defeats. Latin America is awakening from a dream: being able to practice reformism without the possibility of revolution, without the latter constituting a threat to the survival of capitalism.

Thinking that poverty could be reduced and the situation of proletarians could be improved through the mechanisms of "finance" was more than a naiveté or a "paradox": it was a perversion. One cannot make "credit" a mere instrument, adaptable to no matter what political project, since it constitutes the most abstract and the most formidable weapon of capitalism. As always, financialization, introducing the "limitless" (the infinite) into production, led to an economic and political crisis. And as always, the financial crises opened a political phase marked by the logic of war or, more exactly, by a resurgence of class wars and wars of race and gender which, from the beginning, are the founding characteristic of capitalism.

The New Fascisms

> "If [American] conservatives acquire the conviction that they can't win democratically, they won't abandon conservatism. They'll reject democracy."
>
> — David Frum

The new fascisms conquered political hegemony in a dual manner, by declaring a "break" with the neoliberal "system" (more in words than in deeds) and above all by designating the immigrant, the Muslim as the enemy. The political polarizations which the class inequalities haven't ceased to feed, especially since 2008, are, through racism, reconfigured into a phantasmal but "real" people that takes a form and an identity by being set against a common enemy.

Like racism, fascism, and sexism, war changes, transforms. After forty years of neoliberal policies, what is coming will not be a simple repetition of the interwar experience. Neo-fascism results from a twofold mutation: from historical fascism, on one hand, and from the organization of counter-revolutionary political violence, on the other hand. Many hypocritically call this phenomenon "populism." The reasons for "not seeing" are deep, rooted in the modalities of capitalist production and consumption.[7]

Contemporary fascism is a mutation of historical fascism in the sense that it is national-liberal instead of national-socialist. The political movements issuing from '68 are now so weak that it is not even necessary to take up their demands while twisting them, like the fascists and the Nazis did in the 1930s. At the time, "socialist" had in their mouths precisely this meaning and this function: integrating the demands from which the dictatorship removed any revolutionary significance. Nothing of the sort in the new fascism, which, on the contrary, is ultra-liberal. It is for the market, business, individual initiative, even if it wants a strong state, on the one hand, for "repressing" the minorities, the "foreigners," the delinquents, etc., and on the other hand, like the ordoliberals, for literally building the market, business, and above all property. It utilizes democracy, which, without the egalitarian push of revolutions, is an empty shell lending itself to every adventure. The parliamentary regime and elections suit it perfectly, because under these conditions, they are favorable to it. Its racism is "cultural." It no longer has anything "conquering" or imperialist about it, as in the age of colonizations: it would prefer to draw back inside the boundaries of the nation-state. It is defensive, fearful and anxious, rather, conscious that the future is not on its side. Antisemitism has given way to the phobia of Islam and the immigrant.

Historical fascism was one of the modes of actualization of total wars; the type that is growing right before our eyes is, on the contrary, one of the modes of warfare against the population. The new fascism doesn't even have to be "violent," paramilitary, like historical fascism when it was a matter of destroying the worker and peasant organizations militarily, because contemporary political movements, unlike "communism" between the two world wars, are very far from threatening the existence of capital and its society: during the last decades, there have not been any revolutionary political movements in the USA, nor in Europe, nor in Latin America, nor in Asia.

Historical fascism, once the revolutionary forces were annihilated, was the agent of the process of "modernization" (Gramsci) which, "integrating" socialism, repressed through violence every manifestation of conflictuality. In Italy, it restructured the traditional industry and created the film industry, reformed the school system and the civil code (still in force today) and established a welfare state (under the Nazis, this latter was more "radical" than that of the United States). With the new fascisms, the agenda remains that of neoliberalism, combined with nationalism.

The recomposition of the people around its phantasmal unity is very disturbed by the action of gay, lesbian, and transgender subjectivities that escape the majoritarian model which the nostalgia of the neo-fascists would like to reconstruct around heterosexuality. The rise of neo-fascist forces is always accompanied by campaigns of ferocious "hatred" against the so-called "gender theory." Reconstruction of the family and the heterosexual order constitutes the other powerful vector of fascist subjectification.

What the old and the new fascisms share is a core of self-destructiveness and a suicidal desire which capital has transmitted to them: capital is not "production" without at the same time being "destruction" and "self-destruction." After Europe's suicide in the first half of the 20th century. When capitalism had attained the highest degree of its productive forces, are we currently seeing that of America, now that those forces have crossed another threshold of growth? In any case, there is a continuity, a family resemblance that traverses capital and fascism, which the 20th century brought to light and which the 21st century proposes anew, in new forms.

The evolution of this fascist wave is hard to predict: it is characterized by notable internal differences—Erdogan and Bolsonaro, on one side, the European neo-fascists, on the other, with Trump between the two. What can be affirmed with certainty is that the historical fascisms did not resolve the contradictions and impasses of capital. On the contrary, they exacerbated them and in this way they led the world toward the Second World War. Trump is in the process of destabilizing neoliberal capitalism, by undertaking to accelerate the deregulation of finance, strengthen the monopolies of American corporations (the digital companies in particular) and reduce taxes on behalf of a "plutocracy," while claiming to protect the victims of these same deregulations and monopolies (the white working class). To say nothing of his foreign policy.

The revival of fascisms in Europe is not a recent phenomenon. It is parallel with the beginnings of neoliberalism (while in Latin America, fascism was its condition of possibility), because the denunciation of the Fordist compromise of the "Glorious Thirty" required new modes of division, control, and repression. Incited, solicited, organized by the state, the management of racism, sexism, and nationalism passed into the hands of the new fascisms.

In Foucault's view, their global proliferation poses no difficulty: in a certain way, the fascisms have always been there; they belong to the organization of the state and of capital. Foucault calls this "outgrowths of power" which exist virtually "on a permanent basis in Western societies," which are "structural, as it were, intrinsic to our systems and can reveal themselves on the least occasion, making them perpetually possible."[8] He cites as "glaring examples," "the Mussolinian, Hitlerian, Stalinist system," but also Chile and Cambodia. Fascism has only extended "a series of mechanisms that already existed in the social and political system of the West." But while Foucault had a clear grasp of the relationship between the state and fascism, he didn't see their connection with capital, which makes both of them components of its war machine.

It's not just a matter of saying like Primo Levi that if the fascisms, Nazism, took hold this can happen again, but of affirming that the fascisms, racism, sexism, and hierarchies they produce are structurally embedded in the functional mechanisms of capitalist accumulation and the states.

Fascists and the Economy

"Progressive" liberals and "democrats" can't get over the alliance of certain business sectors, and finance first of all, with the new fascisms. One can be surprised about the "return" of the war that financialization always carries along with it only if one persists in imagining capital to be simply a "mode of production."

There is no incompatibility between dictatorships and neoliberalism. Neoliberals are always unambiguous about this. The libertarian Von Mises declared that fascism and the dictatorships saved "European civilization" (by which he meant pivate property), a merit which, according to him, would remain forever engraved in history. As for the ineffable Hayek, he preferred a "liberal dictatorship" to a "democracy without liberalism," for the sake of a private property synonymous with liberty. Pinochet guaranteed that; Allende, not so much.

Contrary to a widely held opinion difficult to eradicate, the fascisms don't constitute obstacles to the economy, to commerce, to finance. In the debates of the French parliament before 1914 the same arguments resounded as today: war is not possible because the interdependences between the national economies are too strong; globalization has penetrated too deeply into production and commerce for war to be possible. We know how that turned out! After the First World War, Italian fascism maintained good relations with Wall Street, despite the economic "autarchy" it claimed and even though the USA, under the pressure of a growing xenophobia, had imposed immigration quotas that affected the Mussolini regime in particular.

"Nationalism," autarchy, xenophobia only concern the internal management of the different populations of the different countries and intervene only marginally in economic affairs at the planetary level. Even if the conjunctures are different, the lesson of the interwar years can still be useful today. "The policies of national economic development are far from being incompatible with the promotion of international commerce and its financial networks. The 'national' in 'international' must be taken seriously. Italy's elites of the business world have never envisaged their country's development separately from the world economy. The immediate effect of the First World War was not so much to give free rein to deglobalization, as it was to reconfigure international economic exchanges."[9] Hoover and Roosevelt, like Churchill, for that matter, expressed themselves very favorably towards Mussolini, who restored order, "modernized" industry and the country, and staved off the Bolshevik danger, the only real danger for all the capitalist elites.

"The agreement on war debts negotiated in 1925 is the most generous agreement that America has concluded with its allies [...]. American investments in Italy quickly surpassed 400 million dollars." When President Hoover set about reviving a global governance, fascist Italy was one of the privileged partners. The harmony of the 1920s between liberals, finance, and fascists was not disrupted because of the intensification of the fascist dictatorship, but by the crisis of 1929. Adam Tooze points out that the history of the relationship of "democracy" and fascism was rewritten and falsified during the Cold War, leaving out the fact that, as early as 1935, institutions as important as JP Morgan collaborated closely with men subsequently treated as fascist criminals."[10]

Once again, one needs to consult Hayek and the reasons he adduces to legitimate the fascisms. Dictatorship—he's speaking of Pinochet—dismantles "political freedoms" and allows "personal freedoms" to proliferate (freedom of the economy, freedom to buy and sell, to start a business, and above all the freedom of finance to invest, to speculate, to loot through economic rent).

The only danger, historically borne out, is that of the autonomization of fascist politics, which may form themselves into independent and self-destructive war machines; but this is a risk that capitalists and liberals have not hesitated to run when private property was in danger and which they will not hesitate to run whenever they deem it necessary. Capital is not just economy, but also power, political project, strategy of political confrontations, the sworn enemy of political revolutions carried out by its "slaves" (workers, poor people, women, colonized subjects). Contrary to another received idea, capital is not "cosmopolitan," and its deterritorialization, its indifference to territories and to its boundaries, is entirely relative. Its objective is to develop the productive forces, but solely on the condition that they produce profit. This condition (Marx laid it out clearly) is in an obvious contradiction with the development "in itself" of science, labor, technology, etc. Profit requires that the reterritorialization that ensures its existence be realized through the nation-state, racism, sexism and if need be war and the fascisms, the only things capable of politically ensuring the continuation of exploitation and spoliation when the situation toughens. It is naïve to think that subordination of the productive forces to profit is purely immanent to the functioning of the economy, law, and technology. Without the state, without war, without racism, without fascism, no profits. The "triumph" over the subaltern classes was not produced once and for all, it must be continually repeated, reproduced.

Contemporary Racism, a Mutation of Colonial Racism

"Well, I'll say this, if you bump into any young or not so young people from the disadvantaged banlieues, tell them for me that if there is one thing this movement has taught me, it's to completely reconsider the way I looked at that 'riffraff' and its alleged violence. For a month and a half now, we have taken a beating once a week, and I am already fed up, so I can't even imagine the anger they must have inside them at undergoing what they undergo or say they do. Anyway, I believe this is the first time that I feel close to them, and I tell myself almost daily that I was an idiot, with my average privileged white man's eyes."

— A Yellow Vest

Historical fascism wasn't the first implementation of the techniques of repressive, destructive, genocidal power. Those techniques first constituted the means for controlling and regulating the colonized. The "regulation" of populations through slavery burgeoned long before the deployment of European biopower and long before its culmination in Nazi Germany. The 'heavy' machine of colonialism has always "maintained between life and death—always closer to death than to life—those who are forced to keep it moving."[11] Nor was the control of populations integrating "racism" as a weapon of hierarchization and segregation invented by the fascisms, but it was widely practiced in the colonies where "race" was invented.

Contemporary racism is a mutation of colonial racism and of the war against the colonized populations. The Black, the Muslim, the migrant are not on the other side of the racial barrier, separated by the sea or ocean. They people the cities of the North as citizens or, often, they work the arduous jobs on the labor market which Westerners don't want to do.

Capitalism is ruled since the conquest of the Americas by a global governance whose main task is the production and reproduction of the division between the populations of the metropole and those of the colonies. The economy-world has been structured on the basis of the racial division that has spread over the planet while serving a function that is political and economic at the same time. A dramatic division, under whose shelter all of European power and knowledge were constituted, as was the workers' movement, which "profited" from that imperialist strategy, as Engels notes for the case of the English workers.

The strength and strategic role of this division literally leaps out, seeing that, starting with the First World War and with an acceleration after the Second World War, it fell under the assault of the anticolonial and anti-imperialist revolutions. Because of its collapse, capital was obliged to change its strategy and transform the *separation between populations of the North and the South* into a *competition between all the populations* of the planet. Globalization is this strategic act of placing labor power in competition on the global scale.

During the whole era of colonization, migrations went from Europe to the rest of the world in order to exploit it and, by exporting populations, to avert European civil wars. At present, the very small percentage of migratory flows that don't go from the South towards the South are enough to destabilize the North, so that the racial divisions of which the migrants are the victims are installed as a means of control of the populations of the North and are added to the segregations that the European citizens of "colonial" origin were already undergoing. Racism, a technique of governmentality on the labor market, will play just as fundamental a role in political governance, where it constitutes one of the powerful mechanisms of nationalist identitarian subjectification.

Against every modernizing conception of colonization, this separation absolutely must be reproduced, so that, if capital can no longer distribute "forced labor" according to the division between colony and metropole, it will try to produce it within the latter. It's for this reason that precarious labor takes the form of "servile labor" and gains, from year to year, new sectors and new strata of the old body of wage earners.

From this point of view, one could affirm that globalization consisted in transferring to the West the heterogeneity of enslavements and dominations that characterized production in the colonies, commanded and controlled by the superior power of finance, rather than a generalization of wage earning, as Marxism envisaged it. The structuring of our societies resembles the colonial reality in a formal sense: "protean, unbalanced, where slavery, serfdom, barter, handicrafts, and stock market operations coexist."[12] Significantly, the geographer

Guy Burgel sees in contemporary France divisions that trace back to the colonial mode of exploitation; "[T]he "periphery" is closer to the third-world analyses of a Celso Furtado or a Samir Amin, that contrasted it in the 1960s to the "center" of the capitalist system, rather than situating it in a simplistic cartography or sociology of territories."[13] "Racial" segregation is a mode of governmentality that certain states (such as Israel) inscribe in their formal constitution, whereas for others (like the USA), it is at the basis of their material constitution from those countries' birth.

The main function of what Foucault calls the "outgrowths of power" is to produce subjugations. Yesterday, that of the "colonized" and the "colonizer," today that of the migrant and the Western racist. Colonialism, while being an exercise of violence, is characterized by a specific form of production of subjectivity. In the same way, contemporary racism ensures a production of subjugation that is peculiar to it.

If it is true, as Foucault emphasizes, that subjugations "are not derived phenomena, the consequences of other economic and social processes," the production of the "racist" maintains a close tie with capitalism, particularly with its most deadly motor, private property. Racism makes it possible to realize the promise that liberalism has always made and will never be able to keep, to turn every individual into a property owner. This is the brilliant intuition of Jean-Paul Sartre, who explains antisemitism in this way. Antisemites, he tells us, "belong to the petty bourgeoisie of the cities [and] and don't own anything. But it's precisely by rising up against the Jew that they suddenly become aware of being owners; by imagining the Israelite as thief, they place themselves in the enviable position of people who might be robbed; since the Jew aims to steal France, it is France that belongs to them. So they have chosen antisemitism as a means of realizing their quality as owners."[14]

The object of hatred and rejection has changed, but the same mechanism remains at work: the migrants, the immigrants, the Muslims, etc, "are stealing our jobs," "our women," "they're invading our territories." The fear of being robbed, fear in general, that powerful affect constitutive of European politics from its beginnings, defines the racist: "It's a man who is afraid. Not of the Jews certainly: of himself, of his consciousness, of his freedom, of his intincts, of his responsibilities, of solitude, of change, of society, and of the world; of everything but Jews."[15] Millions of non-owners and petty proprietors who see the *real* possibility of losing the little they have due to "follies" of the stock market find their material and spiritual "property" in the *phantasmal* affirmation of the Nation, the identity of the supreme people.

The Secession of the Wealthy

"The wealthiest have decided to wage a war against us [...] I frequent rich people in Paris and their indifference is total. If you tell them that in Spain, if you're 60 years old, you may be obliged to work for 2.60 euros an hour, they shrug. You realize that they are already prepared for such a world. In their heads, it's arranged: for the poor, things will be very tough, and they don't give a shit [...] One will live among the wealthy in mini-bubble bunkers. Too bad for the wretches. For a long time I had the impression that the wealthy were just oblivious, but now I think it's worse: it's something agreed upon, it's what they want, that people sink into a bleak poverty. They don't see the worker as a human being but as a problem to be managed."

— Virginie Despentes

The new fascisms limit themselves to reinforcing the hierarchies of race, sex, and class; the political strategy remains neoliberal. The mission of these new fascisms is not to combat an opposition that doesn't exist, but to carry through to the bitter end the political project that is at the root of neoliberal policies.

Contrary to the theories that speak to us of an "exodus" by the multitudes or a "secession" by the people (Rancière), it is capital that is organizing its escape, its "separation" from society. If our "living together" has never been one of the concerns of capital, the latter now seems to affirm straight out the goal it is pursuing in an absolutely conscious way: making itself politically *autonomous* and *independent* of workers, poor people, and non-owners. *Politically* at least, because from the "economic" point of view, it needs them, but like the planter it needs slaves. Neoliberalism has broken with the Fordist pact focused on employment, but the unions and the workers' movement have remained attached to the norms, rules, and rights of labor and social security rights that have been gradually destroyed to be supplanted by non-negotiable and unnegotiated labor relations and relations of servile domination. Gated communities, numerous in Brazil, in the USA and elsewhere, disturbing as they are, are only the folkloric symptom of this vision of "society."

In the USA, the country of the fully deployed neoliberal paradigm, the impoverished "minorities," (Blacks, Hispanics, women), marked out for precarious jobs, parked in residential and education ghettos, deprived of medical and retirement assistance and the object of a ferocious racial war, populate the prisons by the hundreds of thousands. Henceforth, this reality is also the future of the white working class and middle class, hence the success of the politics of Trump, who promises them an impossible social, racial, and sexual supremacy.

In the secessions of the owning class, privatization has transformed insurance policies against the social risks into mechanisms producing growing inequalities. Privatization radically changes the functions of what Foucault calls the apparatuses [*dispositifs*] of "biopower." Since the 1970s, it has set about systematically undoing the political "power" which the populations accumulated in two centuries of revolutionary struggles and nullifying its translation into rights to health care, education, retirement, unemployment compensation, etc.: access to all of that will depend henceforth on property and inheritance.

For the large majority of the planet's population, biopolitics ought to ensure the "vital" minimum necessary to its simple reproduction. In France, where "welfare" should be more resistant than elsewhere, the economic policies have produced the innovation of the "third class," the class of poor people who have a right to transportation, hospital care, and even third-class funerals. Biopolitics divides (into three classes and it individualizes even more subtly), and in dividing, it impoverishes a large majority and enriches a small minority. It produces not human capital, the self-marketer, but the "working poor," by consigning this majority to the condition of "working poverty."

Control and regulation are no longer accomplished through *integration*, but through social *apartheid* (another name for the political secession of capital) rather than through biopolitics. Societies have become patrimonial again. The rentiers reign over them like in the novels of Balzac. As to wages, after having acquired the status of "independent variable" of the economy, they have again become, as before the cycle of revolutions, a mere variable of adjustment of the fluctuations of profit, and tend irresistibly toward the "minimum." But the income inequalities are nothing in comparison with the asset inequalities, fed by a rent that is no longer primarily colonial, but financial.

At the beginning of the 21st century, other events profoundly affected subjectivities already devastated by the first sequence of neoliberal policies. The breakdown of the financial system in 2008 produced a double "subjective" rupture by initiating a more intense phase of instability that was more directly political, favorable to a neofascist conversion of society (or a "revolutionary" radicalization). First, the debt "crisis" confirmed the failure of the figure of the possessive and competitive individualism of "human capital" and brought forth the subjective figure of the "indebted man," responsible for and guilty of public overspending. Second, following an intensification of neoliberal policies of concentration of wealth and asset-harvesting, the frustration, fear, and anxiety of the indebted man produced a conversion of subjectivity, making the latter receptive to neofascist, racist, sexist adventures and to the identitarian and supremacist fundamentalisms.

Contemporary liberalism is thus very far from the irenic image that Michel Foucault gave of the society of the entrepreneur of the self in *The Birth of Biopolitics*; the "exhaustively disciplinary" industrial society will yield to the "optimization of differences," to the "tolerance accorded to minoritarian individuals and practices." This idyllic setup has never seen the light of day anywhere. And just as we are very, very far from an optimization of differences and tolerance accorded to minorities, we're unable to appeal to Jacques Lacan's "discourse of the capitalist," the psychoanalytic version of neoliberal power according to Foucault: power's injunction would no longer be "you must obey," but "you must climax."

Today the climax in question is the one that Trump wants to procure for white Americans when he defends their "whiteness" from the "races" (Blacks, Latinos, Arabs) who are "threatening" it; or again, white people's thrill when the neoconservatives promise to re-establish the power they are said to have lost, along with the order of the family, and heterosexuality. In Europe, it is Islam that is the object of all the paranoid fixations and all the forms of *ressentiment* which liberalism has produced for the past forty years.

The logic of the war against populations and the logic of its expressions (racism, fascism, and sexism) characterize the epoch. The growing intensity of neofascist mobilizations, the free circulation of racist and sexist speech and acts, seem to be able to fit themselves into the framework of neoliberal governmentality without too many problems, because they participate in the same capitalist war machine.

In the framework delineated, on the one hand, by the project of political secession of the "rich" and, on the other, by the powerlessness of the forces that wish to block it, democracy no longer has any utility. Representative democracy did not enter into "crisis" with neoliberalism: the legislative power that is meant to realize it and legitimate it began to be neutralized by executive power as early as the First World War. Industrial war called for a reconfiguration of executive power, which didn't end with the cessation of hostilities, but would gradually reduce Parliament to the status of an appendage for ratifying and legitimating the decrees of the real legislative power, which is in the hands of the executive. But stopping our analysis here would be to stay in the groove traced out by Carl Schmitt or Agamben. The 20th century manifested a new "political" reality which neoliberalism fully actualized: executive power, like the whole juridico-political system, is one of the centers of decision of capital's war machine, which executes, ratifies, and legitimates "decrees" designed to augment financial capital's "life" (its power of acting).

Liberals have always understood democracy as democracy of the wealthy. They've always thought of rights as being indexed to property. It was revolutions that imposed equality and won political and social rights "for all." Capitalism can very well function within different political systems: constitutional democracy, a centralist and authoritarian state as in China, in Russia, or in the fascist regimes. The idea according to which capital necessarily goes hand in hand with democracy has not ceased to be contradicted.

War and Circulation

Beginning with the end of the 1970s, the post-'68 movements stopped questioning and problematizing war, civil war, and revolution. Concepts of war and revolution were abandoned by the "defeated," as if war was completely integrated, incorporated, and pacified in production, democracy, and consumption, and revolution could only merge with technology (automotive, digital, robotic, etc.). "Peace" was confused with the historical victory of capitalism, and the "end" of wars with the defeat of revolution. But it is impossible to comprehend the change in the way capitalism functions, its neoliberal revamp, the emergence of new forms of fascism, without thematizing the victories and defeats of the 20th century, since it was the "triumphs" in the war between classes that opened up the possibility of these transformations.

If, as I believe, the political defeat of the late sixties and early seventies also involved a theoretical defeat, the first victim was Marxism, which had supplied most of its political and theoretical tools to the century of revolutions.

The emergence of political subjects not easily identifiable with the working class (the decolonization movement and the feminist movement, among others) rattled the concept of the revolutionary subject inherent in European Marxism, but the reasons for its rapid collapse, consummated, in the 1970s, are to be sought first of all in the total wars. The Great War had been the occasion of the seizure of power by the Bolsheviks, but also the origin of a radical disruption of the functioning of capitalism, continued by the Second World War and the Cold War, a disruption that Marxism, unlike the capitalists, was not capable of apprehending.

The two total wars deeply affect the Marxian category of "production," the basis of the revolutionary rupture since it engenders the subject that can bring it about. Production came out of the total wars radically different from how Marx had defined it, as did the subjects of "revolution." *It became a part of circulation*, in several ways. Starting in the Cold War, it was no longer more than a moment of the circulation of commodities (logistics) and, with the rise of neoliberalism, a moment of the circulation of money (finance) and the circulation of information (mass media and digital industries). More generally, as the feminist theories have suggested, production is now just one part of "social reproduction." It is subordinate to the possibility and the ability to reproduce and control the whole set of dominations and the strategic confrontations that characterize them.

Logistics brings into focus, perhaps better than finance and information, the continuity between the organization of labor and the organization of war, the strict entanglement between civilian and military that is at the basis of contemporary capitalism and its global market.[16]

Production is pincered between immediately global "circulation" networks, which delineate new dimensions of the space-time of accumulation, and new modes of warfare, which cross through the nation-states and their boundaries. All the networks of circulation of commodities, of money and information, but also all the networks of social reproduction, are strategic centers of the "global social machine"—that is, of the reorganization of national economies into a transnational capitalist machine (which states help to assemble in an indispensable way). Already at the end of the 1950s and the beginning of the 1960s, capitalists viewed "production" in terms of the interconnection between production, distribution, and consumption on the scale of the world market. The capitalists think of "value" and calculate valorization on the basis of the "total cost" of these different integrated flows of circulation and production. Thanks to logistics, the factory is fragmented, spread, stretched between the different territories of the planet, so that a single commodity incorporates a multiplicity of parts from all over the globe. While Marx made the factory the "motor" and the "beginning of the value chain," "commodities today are manufactured *across* logistics space rather than in a single place." (Marxists will have trouble understanding the logic and function of logistics, because its dual origin—on one hand, the slave trade and the circulation of commodities produced in the colonies, and, on the other, war, particularly industrial war—upends their theoretical framework, which is still very industrial and Eurocentric.)

Extensive globalization, which exploits the whole planet, and intensive globalization, which exploits the whole society, are the "civilian" transposition of the "war economy" of the first half of the 20th century. The matrix of contemporary capitalism is located in the globalization of war and the mobilization of all the social forces for the industrial production of destruction which, with the atomic bomb, became virtually "total." The two total wars mark the indissoluble strategic unity of capital and war, of production and power (and first of all the power of the state).

The considerable advantage which capital has gained over labor power has its source at the end of the 1950s and the beginning of the 1960s, when capitalists, by integrating the double socialization of production put in place by the total wars, asked themselves the question: "Where does production end?" The answer to this question was found in the experience of the American army during the Second World War, where in fact production (for the war) had no limits, since it merged with the activity of the "nation" and its space merged with the planet as a whole. As Cowen explains it, "the old military art of logistics played a fundamental role in the construction of the global social machine [...] Business interest in logistics commenced during World War II when immense quantities of materiel had to be strategically deployed throughout the world."

War is not only the genealogical model of the value chain, it is also an indispensable component of the contemporary functioning of the circulation of capital, because the transnational dimension of logistics requires a "security" model that is no longer centered on the nation-state. Rather than a simple militarization of logistics, what is involved is a co-production by the firms and the armies (neoliberalism introduced privatization even in this domain), a new conception of the relation between valorization and "security." The American army made available to civilians the enormous productive, technological, scientific, but also military experience acquired during the total wars and the Cold War. As with financialization, it's always the state that has the initiative and the problem lies in the way in which these capabilities are transferred to the private sphere.

The state and its borders, by defining the nation's "inside" and "outside," established the basis of the divisions between policing action and military action, war and peace, war and terrorism. The transnational functioning of finance and logistics blurs these divisions, particularly between civil and military. The "security" of globalization, reversing the relationship between circulation and production, can only be assured by a combined civilian and military action, distributed between business and (regular and mercenary) armies. "For a system based not simply on connectivity, border security can itself be a source of insecurity for the supply chain." The central concern of the supply chain is protection of the commodity flows and the infrastructures of transport and communication that sustain them.

Logistics (management of the transport of commodities and management of the transport of information) made flexible and just-in-time production possible, and it is always "circulation" that has enabled the global exploitation of a labor force scattered over the whole planet. Exploitation of labor power on a world scale is what defines capitalism, but with logistics, for the first time, it is the result of an integrated "productive," technological, informational, administrative, military-policing machine. Capital, thanks to logistics, juggles between real subsumption and formal subsumption of labor power—that is, between exploitation of highly qualified labor through very heavy investments in fixed capital (machines, technologies, science) and exploitation of servile labor, child labor, slavery, with modalities that don't seem to belong to capitalist modernity. In reality, capitalism combines and holds together, today like before, the most innovative, "capital-intensive" production and the most traditional and violent modes of "labor-intensive" exploitation.

Circulation and Finance

"Debt is still neocolonialism, where the colonizers are transformed into technical assistants. In fact, we ought to say that they're transformed into technical killers. Debt controlled by imperialism is a cleverly organized reconquest to make Africa, its growth, its development obey norms that are completely foreign to us."

— Thomas Sankara, July 29, 1987

What emerges from contemporary circulation is, in many respects, very different from the "security apparatuses" analyzed by Michel Foucault. Like logistics, these security apparatuses according to him have the objective of constantly expanding the circulation circuits by ceaselessly integrating "new elements: production, psychology, behaviors, ways of creating producers, buyers, consumers, importers, exporters, the world market." The Foucauldian confidence in "security apparatuses" ("let circulation take its course, control circulations, sort out the good ones and the bad ones, always keep things moving, perpetually going from one point to another, but in such a way that the dangers inherent in this circulation are neutralized")[18] sounds a lot like the false naïveté of the liberal theoreticians. Capitalists are more circumspect about the nearly automatic capacity of the security apparatuses to neutralize the "dangers" and the "risks." As we've just seen, they think, more prosaically, of security in strict cooperation with the militaries.

This continuous expansion of production via circulation is confronted with so many resistances, refusals, diversions, subtractions, violent organized struggles, individual acts of sabotage, that govern-mentality necessarily implies a relation with the unforeseeable and the unpredictable, what Foucault calls a "relation with the event," with the "series of possible events," with the "temporal" and the "randomness" of conflict. But in capitalism, this relation with the event goes necessarily by way of techniques of warfare, which, by definition, deal with the unforeseeable and the unpredictable.

If we view things from the perspective of globalized production, we have, once again, a vision of neoliberalism very different from the one offered by Michel Foucault in *The Birth of Biopolitics*. The organization of production based on circulation enables capitalism to "optimize the differences" between the statuses of workers and the different "costs of labor power" worldwide— that is, to optimize the heterogeneous modes of exploitation and to profit from the existing dif-ferentials between the systems of social security, between the fiscal and juridical regimes.

The government of this globalized production has its strategic center in finance, whose "commodity," money, circulates at a speed beyond comparison with that of the commodities managed by logistics. Finance, like logistics, maintains a very close relationship with war and particularly with the war against populations, for which it will constitute the most formidable weapon. Indeed, the global market, especially with neoliberalism, doesn't integrate without differentiating through racist, segregationist, sexist techniques; or homogenize without worsening inequalities; or unify without accentuating "wars" between nation-states, wars of class, of sex, and of race.

After the "historical triumph over the subaltern classes" in the 1970s, the international financial institutions began by intervening heavily with a new strategy that recast power relations as relations between creditors and debtors. The debt strategy was first put in place with a twofold objective: to recover what the West had lost because of anticolonial struggles and to discipline the subjectivities formed by the anti-imperialist revolutions which found it difficult to comply with the "development" imperatives of the World Bank.

Sylvia Federici describes this process very precisely. In the 1980s, the World Bank played a central role in Africa, by replacing the "departing colonial administrations" and putting in place a "special program" called "structural adjustment": "In exchange for 'growth-oriented' loans, a country accepts the liberalization of imports, the privatization of state industries, the abolition of all restrictions on currency exchange and commodity prices, the demise of any subsidy program, and the elimination of all workers'rights and social security."[19] These policies of structural adjustment adopted the name of the "Chilean experiment" which they perpetuate.

Between 1970 and 1980, the great international institutions of capital cast blame on "Africa's resistance to development," because despite the political defeat the anti-imperialist revolutions solidified a refusal expressed in behaviors hindering the objectives of capital. "The difficulty which African proletarians had accepting the laws of capital as natural laws, is especially pronounced among the new generations that grew up during the period of intense liberation struggles."[20]

The "programming of the debt crisis affected, from the beginning of the 1980s, more than 25 African countries." It was the means of "recolonizing a large part of the former colonial world, plunging whole regions into debt and reducing them to poverty. Because of the debt crisis, the successes obtained with the anticolonial struggle were nullified."[21] The debt economy proved so effective as an instrument of recolonization and imposition of capitalist norms on the "third world" that its mechanisms were extended to North American workers and later to Europeans.[22]

The collective capitalist constructs his war machine on the basis of circulation; so there is no exteriority, no parasitic function of finance vis-à-vis the "real economy": on the contrary, thanks to its greater degree of deterritorialization, thanks to its speed and its constant acceleration, it has a vision of the overall cycle of "production." Once freed from the political constraints that had been imposed on it in the 20th century because of the destructive power it had unleashed, once delivered over to its logic of "no limits," of "always more," its greater deterritorialization made it into the privileged site of command and strategy, but also the source of wars and, with them, strategic confrontations.

Military Minds and War after the Cold War

War, both as a productive force and as a force for the political conversion of capitalism, underwent profound transformations throughout the 20th century, which the critics of capitalism, holding that war is not part of capitalism's organization, completely overlook.[23] Among the new definitions that military strategists produced after the fall of the Soviet Union, "war against the population" strikes me as the best notion for explaining not only the military strategies, but also the strategies behind the policies of neoliberalism. Both marry, in a different way, the civil and the military, and find their point of convergence in the war against populations.

Although military thinkers are sometimes more attentive than critical intellectuals to the transformations of capitalism, they overlook, like the intellectuals, a fundamental political phenomenon: the defeat of revolution. The Cold War was the framework in which (with the participation of the US and Soviet powers, and more often, despite and against them) a "global civil war" unfolded, variously described by Arendt, Koselleck, Schmitt, in which, in reality, the "world revolution" was pitted against the war machine of capital. It is in the defeat of this revolution that the reasons for the transformations of warfare are to be sought.

After the industrial wars of the first half of the 20th century, war and the state started to become functions and components of capital's war machine. "Seizure," "conquest," and appropriation were no longer the exclusive prerogatives of the state, which also lost "the monopoly on violence and its use." If it was also a matter of imposing one's own will by force, the means of constraint were diversified (economic, cultural, social, technological). Force was increasingly exerted by "civilian" subjects. "There are private armies, companies of mercenaries and there are economic and social instruments, just as effective as large-scale bombardments."[24]

The reversibility of war and power returns as a leitmotif in the work of the military strategists and finds in finance the very example of the imposition of constraint by economic force. Finance combines the most deterritorialized form of capital and the most deterritorialized form of sovereignty, war. It "succeeds in destroying the economies of the weak countries, by creating as many victims as a battle."[25]

In no case does this involve the disappearance of the state, but rather its integration into a strategy, that of capital, which the state is no longer able to elaborate and control as an autonomous and independent power. It exercises its "power" in a "partnership" with other forces that overrun it and subject it to their strategies. What all the strategic theories emphasize is the fact that the "destructive" effects of force can very well have an economic and above all financial origin.

When military strategists consider war nowadays, they don't think of the "front," of regular armies, of confrontations between states as in the period of the total wars that have colonized our imagination. The fronts and the boundaries move about, become internalized within the territory of the pacified states, since military and civil blend together. And their strategic object is the global population.

Total war changed into global war, in the sense that it constitutes the other face of globalization, the military aspect of the "civil" action of the world market. It is endemic, intermittent, always ready to break out, but against a background of war against the population. The war in Syria, the war for the control and "final elimination" of migrants, the war for the privatization of welfare, are certainly not the same, but there does exist a continuity between them, a political transversality: in contemporary capitalism, war is always, at bottom, a civil war, a war against the population. Capital's war, unlike the war waged by the state, does not have as its basis and objective the affirmation and extension of sovereignty, but the submission of humans and non-humans to the production of value. It's only under the political hegemony of capital that the global civil war is prioritized over the war between states. While it's not a matter of a Schmittian war (state, people, destiny), the war machine of capital finds its *enemy* when submission to the laws of production and governmentality flips over into revolution. The expansion of the global war is equal to that of the global market; so it doesn't suffice that one doesn't have any armed conflict on one's soil to be able to say "we are not at war" (this affirmation is a reflex inherited from the colonial era: when one noted that Europe was going through a period of peace, one did so without taking into account the wars that Europeans were conducting in the colonies).

"It is true that war is armed conflict, but the arms are no longer just those known as such [...]. The conflict must be actual, but the signals of this situation are not just military [...] The conflict must be extensive, but the extent" can be measured only by "the effects the conflict has on sovereignty and on the functioning of the political communities involved [...]. Mistakenness about the extent is what allows all the Nato countries not to feel they're at war, while their troops are fighting all over the planet."[26] We re-encounter in the definition of contemporary war all the characteristics of the two world wars. "War, from being an exceptional phenomenon, limited in time, space, and means, has become total, asymmetric and perpetual."

Michel Foucault, in the period (1971–1976) when he was still trying to approach the social relation through "civil war," but without taking into consideration the two world wars and the European civil wars of the 20th century, arrives, in an interview where he plays the part of interviewer, at the same conclusions as the military analysts: "The problem would really be in knowing whether the role of the army is indeed to wage war. Because, if you look closely, you notice that in the end the more the army in history specialized as an army, the more, at the same time, wars ceased to be the business of armies and became a political, economic, etc. phenomenon which enveloped the total body of the population."[27]

The concept of population brings out a political differend with Foucault, whose positioning seems to me to be a symptom of the political sensibility of a particular, post-'68 epoch. During most of the 20th century, the political problem was not that of the population and its "life," but that of the classes, the colonized "nations," and their revolutions (even in the Nazi war against "Judeo-Bolshevism," Jews were "fantasized" enemies, the real political danger coming from the Russian Revolution).[28] The victory of capital transforms the armed class or nation into a "population"—that is, into working masses, jobless dependents, psychotics, migrants, etc. who all become "dangerous" again for lack of being revolutionaries. It's only under the conditions of a defeat of the revolution that civil war can become governmentality—that is, "war within the population" where the places of the winners and the losers are already distributed.

The transformation of global civil war into biopolitics ("war within the population") turns the latter into a war without the "enemy," since the enemy has disappeared with the revolution. With the dissolution of class into the category of population, what power sees everywhere, less as revolution than as "danger," "risk," source of "chaos," is the "terrorist." Since this war coincides with control of the population, it has neither a beginning nor an end. Similarly, it foresees neither a victory nor a defeat since the force relations are asymmetrically established and stabilized for the sake of capital. There is no enemy to be defeated, only losers to be governed and terrorists to be neutralized. At any time, the loser can become a political enemy, provided the subordination to biopolitics and governmentality is transformed into a strategic confrontation. On this unstable ground, "security techniques" intervene with a view to anticipating what can't be anticipated (the event of rupture) and their interventions proliferate precisely because of that impossibility.

The global war, as a war against the population, doesn't know any peace. Or rather, peace becomes a "continuation of war by other means."[29] The interlinking of war and power in Foucault prior to the conceptualization of biopolitics and governmentality does without peace, exactly like the theorization of the military and the civil in military writings after 1989. Through these categories, Foucault and the military theorists register a change that unfolded after the Second World War, but that would be further accentuated with neoliberalism: victory no longer leads to a period of "peace," but on the contrary to the reinstatement of instability (in the same way that economic "crisis" becomes permanent rather than conjunctural).

Defining war by excluding peace as its opposite implies a critique of the dialectical conception of war that is a characteristic of revolutionary Marxism. In Mao, war and peace were still the exemplification of a dialectical relation in which the "identity of contraries" contained the possibility of the reversal of each term. However, at least starting with the Cold War, war and peace ceased to oppose each other dialectically, to convert into one another and the adversaries ceased to face off as contraries/identicals. The negative was no longer dialectizable. The negative remained negative. A radical instability took hold.

Hence the need to think the techniques of governmentality that combine the civil and the military, war and power as a "war against populations." The police is the institution most capable of managing this situation, since the lack of distinction between peace and war, violence and law is there at its foundation: "Therefore, the police intervene 'for security reasons' in countless cases where no clear legal situation exists, when they are not merely, without the slightest relation to legal ends, accompanying the citizen as a brutal encumbrance through a life regulated by ordinances, or simply supervising him."[30]

The remarkable innovation consists in the steering and governance of this war, which the neoliberal capitalist elites cede or are forced to cede to the new fascists. The mutation of fascism that has occurred with neoliberalism is synonymous with a new transformation of war against the population, whose intensity will depend on the strength of the resistances that oppose it. If historical fascism was a continuation of total war, the new fascism is characterized instead by the forms of warfare within the populations.

"Pacification" in the Concept of "Power"

> "Like the outcome, the origin of every contract also points to violence. It need not be directly present in it as lawmaking violence, but is represented in it insofar as the power that guarantees a legal contract is, in turn, of violent origin even if violence is not introduced into the contract itself. When the consciousness of the latent violence in a legal institution disappears, the institution falls into decay."
>
> — Walter Benjamin

One's judgment about wars implies a judgment about capitalism and the struggles waged within it, because in the final analysis every war is a civil war. In practically all the instances of post-'68 political thought, capitalism and power are conceived independently of (civil) war, which excludes, in principle, any possibility of rethinking revolution, but also fascism, racism, and sexism as articulations of war.

Paradoxically, contemporary critical thought takes part in a pacification of the strategic confrontation of the 20th century. Faced with the new configuration determined by capital's victory over revolution, it oscillates between an "analysis of capitalism" that has a hard time integrating the co-penetration of the civil and the military (the near-entirety of "68 thought" fits this case) and an analysis which, like that of Foucault, integrates power and war during a short period, but reveals itself to be incapable of seeing that war is only one component of capital's machine. The conceptions of power that we've inherited from these theories have much to do with the inability to grasp the capitalist strategy and the rise of the new fascisms.

If Foucault is the one who did the most to renew the category of power, he is also the one who is farthest removed from its real functioning in neoliberalism, by obscuring, through the concept of governmentality, the violence that neoliberalism directly exerts on persons and things. His non-juridical conception of a power rooted in the microphysics of relations that constitute the fabric of everyday life has had a significant influence on the theoretical and political elaboration of the new social movements. The concepts of "biopower," "biopolitics," and then "governmentality" have met with a growing success because they appear to be an alternative to the concept and practices of "governance," a mantra of neoliberalism.

It's important to come back to these concepts because, by excluding war and revolution, Foucault makes biopolitics, as his research progresses, an apparatus centered on the augmentation of life and of the power of populations, a control technique that has lost any negative character (violence, repression, war) to define itself as a positive force of production of subjects, freedom, and security. Thanato-politics (the underside of biopolitics and a concept moreover that was never really established) will gradually disappear, replaced by "governmentality," which, giving a general framework to the techniques of management of life, erases what still remained of war in his analyses.

The insistence with which Foucault defines the techniques of power as being "productive," while putting us on guard against any conception of "repressive," destructive, warlike power doesn't correspond in any way to the experience we have of neoliberalism. The fact is, especially since the end of the last century, that war, the fascisms, racism, sexism, nationalism, and neoliberal "reforms" have demonstrated the "negative," repressive, and destructive nature of power.

Deleuze observes that power relations in Foucault differ from simple violence. Power doesn't act upon the person, but on their action, on their "possibilities," which is to say that it is exercised by structuring the field of behavior. It keeps the "subject" on which it is exercised "free," capable of reacting and responding to its solicitations. In contrast, violence acts upon things and persons by closing off all possibilities. Power is not at all "doing violence" or "repressing"; it is rather encouraging, eliciting, soliciting. This is true, no doubt, but only covers a part of power relations, those which *The Birth of Biopolitics* attributes to neoliberalism. And this analysis doesn't correspond to the positions of the neoliberal leaders, who, as we've seen, are far from overlooking the need for the fascisms, dictatorships, and wars to secure freedom ("private property").

The specifically capitalist power of workplace discipline, for example, doesn't focus on "offense and damage," affirms Foucault, but on "potential behavior."[31] It intervenes as it were even before the behavior is manifested. In a similar way, biopolitical techniques act where things will occur, "depending on possible events or a series of possible events."[32] Power consists in the fact of "probalization." This is exactly the kind of talk that one hears today in the great corporations of Silicon Valley (Google, Amazon, Facebook, etc.): depending on the "data," they will act upon the possible behaviors by anticipating them.

But if one sticks to this definition, one has a truncated vision of the exercise of power. The latter is not limited to exerting an action upon another action, it also involves the possibility of imposing its will through force, through violence, through an action that, instead of acting on another action, acts directly on persons and things (non-humans). In the workplace as well as in the biopolitical techniques, the two types of violence (acting upon the potentiality of behaviors and acting upon things and persons) coexist, as those who undergo them (workers, migrants, women, etc.) know very well. Capital is not production without also being at the same time destruction, destruction of persons, things, and life forms. If one stops the analysis at "action upon an action" one will thus have a "modernizing" and limited conception of power in capitalism, since its existence and its reproduction also presuppose class, racial, and sexual violences. These relations, which pertain just as much to the "nature" of capitalism, do not belong to a past destined to disappear with the full development of capitalist techniques of power. In order to function, the latter need violence upon things and persons.

Let's take for example the Foucauldian reading of Gary Becker, said to be a great innovator, a modernizer in matters of penal and carceral policies, in perfect harmony with the exit of our societies from the era of "disciplines" and their entry into a period of "soft power." "Society does not need to conform to an exhaustive disciplinary system,"[33] and the penal policy must answer new questions: "What must be tolerated as far as crime goes?" "What would it be intolerable not to tolerate?" This new problematization of delinquency leads to a new methodology which the neoliberals found in economic science and which Foucault sums up in this way: "Penal action must be an action upon the game of possible gains and losses" which the criminal would calculate in "response" to the changes in penal policy established by the governmentality.

Becker's argument (the criminal behaves with a view to maximizing "profit") is simply ludicrous given the reality of forty years of *repressive* policies that produced the greatest "disciplinary" confinement in the history of humanity. In the USA, the prison population has quintupled since the 1970s. American prisoners represent nearly 25% (2.2 million persons) of the global prison population, whereas the country accounts for 5% of the total population. The United States has practiced a mass incarceration that doesn't meet the innovative criteria of "human capital," but, more prosaically, corresponds to the policy of "racial war" that is at the basis of the American material constitution and that neoliberalism reactivated in the most general framework of class war, in order to restore the power of the "economy." One could apply the same critique to "human capital," whose true objective is to reconfigure the labor capacity of wage earners so that it alone will take on the risks and costs resulting from its activity. Individualization, impoverishment, and guilt generation are what rules the politics of "human capital."

Furthermore, the "productive" conception of power defended by Foucault can lead to political misunderstandings, for instance to the illusion of a clash conceived in a one-sided way, as performative against performative (Butler), production against production (Negri), creation against creation (Guattari). To escape from the dialectic of the negative, one abandons war and revolution, which, in themselves, have nothing negative about them. This "positive," "productive" way, inviting one to rethink power, has spawned a politicization that has the look of its opposite instead. For a long time, what has faded from view is not so much the negative modalities of power, but, in a subtle way, all problematization of revolution. It's not a question of saying that the thought of "govern-mentality" is compatible with the "governance" of liberalism, but that it accepts its principal belief: the economy, the institutions, the relations of governors/governed have replaced war, and the impersonal nature of their functioning has replaced strategy.

As for the concept of war, it must not be understood only as armed confrontation between enemies, nor only as strategy. It must also be understood as a critique addressed to the Marxian conception which interprets, in a unilateral way, the power of capital as a supersession of the personal domination peculiar to feudal societies. War doesn't disappear, it cannot be absorbed into the depersonalizing apparatuses of economy and law, because *it is the most glaring manifestation of the fact that power is also violence against persons and things.*

Félix Guattari illustrates this major flaw of '68 thought, by extending for contemporary capitalism Marx's perspective on the power of capital as depersonalization: "Personological relationships of the type noble-valet, master-apprentice fade off, making way for a regulation of general human relations, based mainly on systems of abstract quantification having to do with wages, "qualification," profit."[34] The apparatuses that depersonalize power relations (money, wages, etc.) cannot function without personal relations of power. The Marxian fetishism (relations of power between men turned into relations of power between things) is a source of misunderstandings, since a flow of war, without a flow of racist, sexist, nationalist violence, the abstract and impersonal flows of money, law, etc., would have no chance of being operational.

Negri and Hardt, aligned with these positions that had become dominant after the 1970s, denounce the theories announcing the coming of "new imperialisms" and other "new fascisms" as a "a kind of apocalyptic vision."[35] They veil and mystify the real forms of power that actually dominate our lives—that is, power embodied in property and capital, the power immanent to law and its institutions. Useless to attribute a "dramatic or demonic" form to power, which is excercised, much more normally, by the form of law and property. In this way, the tragic vision characterizing the 20th century is dissipated: "political power is immanent to the economic and juridical structures." Such apocalyptic visions, labeled "*gauchistes*," are even said to be an obstacle to political engagement against the real powers of capitalism, since they imply an inability to "transform in a democratic manner. One must oppose and destroy them, and that is all."

After having updated, following the events of 2011, the "world civil war" by calling it "global" (but without ever making it a constituent component of capital, which for them remains essentially "production"), Negri and Hardt also abandon the concept of war. It seems that at the turn of the century, capitalism hesitated between the option of finance and the option of war, but finally chose the first because "a society in a state of war" can only function for a short time. In the medium term, war undermines "productivity, especially in an economy where freedom, communication, and social interactions are absolutely necessary."

War is anti-economic, affirm Negri and Hardt against all evidence, whereas international finance, like local finance, doesn't hesitate to give its support and lend its men (the bankers of Goldman Sachs) to the "apocalyptic" visions of Trump, or to legitimize and finance a fascist like Bolsonaro. After the total wars, war became, to speak like Marx, one the "principal productive forces," constitutive of "big science," peak technology, and logistics; moreover, it forms since the beginning of the century an indispensable economic sector in constant expansion.

Negri and Hardt radicalize their positions further. Power is not just incorporated into the economy and the law; it is also exercised through automatic mechanisms (norms, technological and scientific protocols) that make the subjectivity of command impersonal, objective, "pacified." "It is even difficult to recognize this [command] as violence because it is so normalized and its force is applied so impersonally."[36] Capitalist control and exploitation are not exercised by an "external sovereign power," but by "invisible" and "internalized" laws. We have left societies of sovereignty behind, since power is immanent to the disciplinary and control apparatuses, which now function in an automatic and impersonal way: money and social norms, digital technology and techniques of governmentality shape our behaviors and our subjectivities, producing habits without resorting to war, coercion, and violence.

Today it seems hard to grasp what Walter Benjamin had remarkably seen between the two world wars. And yet, from neoliberalism's establishment, a "violence that founds" a new economy, a new set of laws, and new institutions was at work, while their operation would be ensured by a violence that "preserved" them—a violence that was often "latent," an "administrative" violence no less effective that the founding violence. Capital's "triumph" over the subaltern classes is not achieved once and for all. It must be reproduced on a daily basis. Given the inability of capitalist forces to overcome the financial breakdown which they themselves caused, the "violence that preserves" must cross a threshold. This is currently taking the form of the new fascisms. Preservation risks degenerating into self-destruction, like what occurred between the two total wars.

At a deeper level still, the founding volence and the preserving violence do not succeed one another; anomie (the suspension of law) and the norm (the production of law) are not two successive moments in the organization of the political order. We are not living in a "permanent state of exception," but more perversely, we're seeing a blurring of the distinction between state of exception and State of law. In France after the attacks of November 2015, the government declared a "state of emergency" that was never revoked; instead, some of its provisions were incoporated into the constitution. The "anti-riot" law (the fourth security law since Emmanuel Macron's arrival at the Élysée) passed in February 2019 against the mobilizations of the "yellow vests" continues to reinforce this hybridization between State of law and state of emergency. "Today, the government and the police forces are re-employing the same mechanisms to maintain public order, no longer against terrorists, but against disturbers or those who appear to be troublemakers. It is clear how once it has been put in our law, the exception spreads and becomes the rule."[37]

In periods of strong mobilization, the State of law and its judicial power see themselves stripped of their prerogatives: these are concentrated in the police ("Sometimes too, the government gives the impression of becoming the hostage of its own police," says François Sureau, a lawyer close to Macron)[38] and in the administration, which, in an arbitrary and definitive way, decides who has the right and the freedom to demonstrate. These decisions made in the "emergency" are never revoked.

The capitalist foundation of the contemporary powers must be underscored once again. Agamben, who tries to combine Carl Schmitt's state of exception with Benjamin's political theology and Foucault's biopolitics, misses what's essential in the transformations of political power, because the "violence that founds" and the "violence that preserves" is no longer the affair of the state, but that of capital.

The passage from anomie to "nomos" is now a prerogative of capital, in a dual manner: either through the intervention of the state, whose two functions of "sovereignty" and "governmentality" are at the diposal of capital, or directly, though the multinationals. In reality, capital is continually in the process of destroying or producing law, of suspending it and activating it, so that we are living in a zone of indistinction. And if this indistinction is what defines the state of exception, the State is definitely not the authority that decides matters today.

"No power without a series of aims and objectives" says Foucault, who adds: the "choices and decisions" don't issue from an "individual subject," nor from a "general staff." But if the aims and decisions no longer belong to the state but to capital, its objectives and its choices, while being those of a machine and not an "individual subject," do resemble more and more the resolutions of a general staff. Thanks to the incredible concentration of production, commerce, estates and wealth, the "committee that administers the common affairs of the bourgeoisie," which the *Communist Manifesto* spoke of, seems to have installed itself in the middle of financial capital.

The state, as the "model of political unity," as the holder of the monopoly on political decision," is "in the process of being dethroned," wrote Schmitt in 1922. This process, begun with the total wars, has come to its end: the monopoly on political decision is now held by capital's war machine. This major event of the 20th century, the subordination of the state and its functions of sovereignty and governmentality to capital, is not explained by Foucault's biopolitics nor by the new versions of it put forward by Esposito and Agamben (the "economic theology" of the Church Fathers is very far from being able to account for the nature and action of capital, to say the least).[39]

What is more, in its understanding of the operation of power such critical thought is betrayed by its "Eurocentrism." It is difficult to think "European civilization" without tying it to war and law, without combining the *unlimited* of strategic confrontation between states (and internal civil wars) and the *limited* of the regulation of those wars by sovereignty, constitutionalism, and governmentality. This regulation is based on an apparatus that is almost never highlighted by political philosophy and the theory of law since, in order to grasp it, one must not lose sight of the "world market" and the global domination that Europe exercised for centuries. Colonialism was not just a formidable machine for exploiting a labor power reduced to slavery. The colonies were not solely lands for plunder, for the accumulation of wealth for Europe. *Colonialism and the colonies were integral and constituent parts of the Western political order.* Competition between the European states, which always risked degenerating into the unlimited of war, stabilized when this division between war and law, unlimited and limited was superimposed on a geographic division between colony and home country. Force, war, the unlimited of violence beyond the color line, in the colonies; law, the limited, sovereignty, constitutionalism in the "civilized world," in the West. A duality that Fanon translates by the couple "colonial violence"/ "peaceful violence"—the oxymoron is only apparent—whose terms maintain "a kind of complicit correspondence, a homogeneity."[40] (Let us note in passing that the Foucauldian correction of the concept of power skips over colonialism as a constituent part of the political order, on the presupposition of sovereignty, governmentality, and constitutionalism, so that his definition of power, while shedding light on power's microphysical dimension, is blind to the global configuration of its macrophysics.)

The two world wars and the process of decolonization triggered by the Soviet revolution exploded this structuration of the Western political order. The total wars imported the limitless violence exerted in the colonies into the confrontation between imperialisms for the "dividing up" of the population of slaves (this is how Lenin defined the struggle for global hegemony between Western powers). Decolonization, in its turn, made inoperative the foundation of that political order by attacking precisely the line of division between "civilization" and "barbarism." The Soviet revolution made it possible, for seventy years, to reconstruct borders, separations, enemies, and civilizational struggles on a new East/West front under whose shelter the constitutional order of the "free world" was also able to reproduce itself.

With the fall of communism, the separation, the borders, the enemy, and the civilizational struggle are being reconfigured and renamed in terms of the old separation between North and South, but in a completely new geopolitical situation. To secure its political order the North is futilely trying to re-establish the "color line." The new fascism is taking on this mission impossible.

Contemporary Power

While the attempt to re-establish the color line is bound to fail, it helps us understand the operation of contemporary power, since the terms it means to separate—order and disorder, war and law, unlimited and limited—are now indissolubly merged.

The nature of contemporary power is manifested unambiguously in the management of migration flows, where we find a new version of the interchange between civil and military. In the waters of the Mediterranean, the "civil" acts in close collaboration with the "military" and both collaborate in concert with armed bands, private armies, organized criminals, drug traffickers, traffickers of human beings, traffickers of organs. Logistics had largely anticipated this situation, but the interconnectedness with corruption and criminality is specific to neoliberalism.

It is very significant that the political crystallizations in the West occur along this neocolonial line and that the "enemy" is a transformation of the colonized. The imbrication of civil and military attempts to reconstruct the line, knowing all the while that it breaks apart in place after place, since the movements of populations are not determined only by contingent reasons (poverty, wars, etc., fueled by the Western capitalists for strategic and economic reasons—plunder of raw materials, land purchases, arms sales), but, more deeply, by the anti-colonial revolutions that formed subjectivities resistant to the neoliberal order. The insistence on autonomy and independence of the struggles against imperialism became embodied in behaviors, attitudes, ways of living which the North's military reptression will have a hard time stopping at its borders.

The border traversing the Mediterranean is mostly phantasmal. Borders have multiplied and fractalized; they have penetrated deep into the Western territories by following the migratory movements they are meant to control and impede (detention centers). They are manifested through all the techniques of spatial segregation that are applied not just to the immigrants, but also to growing parts of the local population (banlieues, ghettos, favelas, etc.). The official border, powerless to hold back the movements of populations, has a very precise function, however, in constituting the locus of subjectification of the new fascisms.

The control of flows and the hierarchization of populations is not accomplished by means of the biopower described by Foucault, nor by its underside, thanato-politics—too generic a term with quasi-metaphysical connotations—but by the war against populations. This expression seems more fitting because it traces a continuity between the physical suppression (of migrants), the new modes of exploitation of labor power, the segregationist policies, the privatization of welfare, etc. Thanato-politics contains the idea of a unilateral power, a pure power of capital, whereas the concept of war implies the relation between (potential or real) enemies.

Sovereign power ("cause to die and let live") and *biopolitics* ("make live and let die") were not successive; they coexist, as one notes today, where the "causing-to-die" (in the case of migrants) is practiced by the same ones who organize the "letting-live" (it would be more exact to say "letting-survive") of nationals. Civil and military, war and governmentality are techniques that operate in tandem, without going by way of peace.

The Foucauldian conception of power is a good example of the limits that affect the thought of '68 in its entirety. While constituting a rupture with respect to classical and even Marxist theories, it shares with them a vision of the operation of power apparatuses centered on the North. In Foucault, half of the genealogical "narrative" concerning the "powers," the political "subjects" and the institutions, is lacking, since the analysis confines itself to Europe. Biopower represents a Eurocentric point of view on apparatuses of power globalized, after all, since 1492. If one analyzes the regulation and control of populations from the standpoint of the economy-world, one can affirm that the war of con-quest, the "military" victory over the "populations," precedes and founds the governmental regulation of those same populations, even in Europe.

Foucault's statement that "the old power of death in which the sovereign power was symbolized is now carefully covered over by the administration of bodies and the calculating management of life" is manifestly false, or at least limited in scope. From the viewpoint of the "world market," this power of death never ceased being exercised, even in Europe, where it produced the horrific mas-sacres of the first half of the 20th century, and it is currently gathering new strength.

Biopolitics and Capital: Of What Life Is It a Question?

Among the concepts of '68 thought, biopolitics has doubtless yielded the richest legacy. It inaugu-rated a veritable field of research, mobilized thousands of students, and it remains a lively ele-ment of our debates (at least the academic ones). It is problematic nonetheless, down to its etymology. Neither racism nor what Foucault calls biopolitics necessarily have a biological basis. The naturaliza-tion of hierarchies based on biological differences (race, the body, sex) is contingent, historical.

Giorgio Agamben and Roberto Esposito, who pride themselves on having gone beyond the limits of the Foucauldian analysis, haven't grasped the watershed represented by the struggles of the 1960s and 1970s: the "naturalness" of racial and sexual differences was undone by the critique conducted by the struggles of the colonized and the feminist struggles. Biopouvoir is not the general form of contemporary power; there does not exist a "biopolitical regime" at the center of contemporary power (Esposito).

"The reversal of the historical into the biological [...] in the thinking about social war"[41] by which Foucault characterizes Nazism is itself historical, contingent. It will be reversed in turn by the struggles of the second half of the 20th century and, as Donatella di Cesare has explained, the "biological" character of Nazi racism itself has to be relativized.[42] In contemporary capitalism, racism and biopower do not necessarily have a biological ground either; and yet they keep producing their "effects of power." Today race doesn't exist biologically, genetically, but it persists as a technique of division, segregation, inferiorization. "Racism without race" continues to produce its political, warlike, and military, effects. Similarly, the body, sex, the reproduction of life have been restored to their reality as political and historical constructions by the feminist movements, which appropriate "biological differences" and systematically transform them into political focuses. The feminist movements constantly politicize what power naturalizes, by problematizing not only gender, the feminine functions and roles, but also sex, the last retrenchment of the heterosexual in the biological.

As we have seen, the military thinkers, in their strategic analysis after the Cold War, also apply a twist to the biopolitical regulation of populations, by separating it from its "biological" grounding. They affirm that future conflicts will be dominated by "war in the midst of populations," the populations having "become both actors and strategic stakes." "The target is much less the state than the population," and winning the war means "controlling the environment" where the populations live. The population, the object of biopolitics, is not understood from the "biological" or "racial" viewpoint, but in its political, social, and historical dimension. Biopolitics, properly so called, is subordinated to war, and civil war constitutes its truth. The enemy thus reverts to being what he always was: a political enemy, even when he expressed his hostility in "racial" terms.

What governmentality must manage first of all is conflict in general and, in particular, the perspective of revolution, whose nature is not biological. In the same way, the life of which it is a question in contemporary biopolitics is the political life of capital. By setting the "political economy of power" against the Marxian "critique of political economy," Foucault makes it more difficult to comprehend the transformations of the exercise of power that occurred starting in the first half of the 20th century, where those two economies became deeply intertwined, and did so under capital's hegemony. The primacy of the "political economy of power" over the "critique of political economy" is an obvious error of the post-'68 interpretation of capitalism, shared moreover by all the philosophers of his generation (Lyotard, Deleuze, Derrida, Guattari, etc. and which one finds repeated, as is, by critical thought, in particular by certain feminist currents. For example, the debate between Nancy Fraser and Judith Butler, with its terms clumsily rendered by the contrast between "social politics" (political economy) and "identity politics" (political economy of power), also derives from that baleful opposition.

At the time (1979) when Foucault declares that the problem of capital accumulation producing wealth and poverty simultaneously is, although it persists, a problem of the 19th century, the machine of capital is showing its intention to recenter its strategy *precisely* on the "limitless" increase in the simultaneous creation of wealth and poverty. The polarization of holdings and incomes is reaching levels that will soon equal or surpass the wealth inequalities produced by capitalism in the 19th century to attain (in the USA) those prior to the French Revolution, while driving the exploitation of non-human life to its breaking point (ecological crisis).

But for Foucault, the urgency is completely different. The priority of political action should be focused on the modalities of subjugation. The struggles and resisistances, he will say at the end of the 1970s, should have as their objective the "effects of power" themselves, on bodies, on subjectivity, rather than on something like exploitation, something like economic inequalities. What must be combated politically "is the fact that a certain power is exercised" because "the fact that it is exercised is intolerable."[43] During that entire decade, Foucault is obsessed by the question of "too much power," of the "excess of power," which will have a definite usefulness for analyzing the development of certain modes of operation of capitalism which Marxism had left aside (prisons, schools, hospitals, etc.) and new forms of fascism, racism, and sexism, but reveals itself to be an impasse when the critique of these "outgrowths of power" is not strictly linked to capitalism's war strategy, producing both wealth and poverty.

While proceeding from a critique of power centered on the juridical to a Nietzschean critique of power, based on "forces," Foucault continues to grant a strategic role to the state. Biopolitics can only be conceived as "a bio-regulation by the state"[44] because, unlike the disciplines, it requires "complex organs of coordination and centralization" which only the state administration can guarantee. But the state, with a view precisely to the organization of this biopolitics, initiates a transformation that will gradually erode its "autonomy" and, in neoliberalism, will turn it into a mere function of capital. But this is what Foucault doesn't see: the discontinuity that revolutionary ruptures entail for the state, on the one hand, and the jumps imposed by capital on the other.

For a long time, even in Europe, there was absolutely no concern for the "life" or death of "proletarians," as Foucault himself recognizes: "The living conditions that were forced on the proletariat, especially in the first half of the 19th century, show that one was far from taking its body and its sex into consideration." It was the danger represented by revolution throughout the 19th and 20th centuries that obliged capital to adopt a strategy of integration, which was always at the same time a technique of division: a division, first, between metropole and colony (whether the colonized lived or died continued to have no importance), and a division within the prolerariat in the home countries. For the life and death of "those people" to become a problem, "it took conflicts [...] it took economic urgencies,"[45] as Foucault rightly remarks. To try and understand the strategy of biopolitics, therefore, it is necessary to place political "life" back at the center of the problematization or, more exactly, to reaffirm the possibility and reality of "revolution" which has haunted the planet for two centuries and which constitutes the true reason for war and the generalization of welfare.

But today the "biopolitical" apparatuses no longer seem to serve the Foucauldian function of augmenting the life of populations. The life that is at stake is not primarily the biological life of the population, but the political life of the capitalist machine and the elites that are its subjectification. Their safeguard necessarily implies the endangerment of the life of populations. To perpetuate that machinic life and its replication, capital is prepared to sacrifice, with no compunction, the health, education, reproduction, housing of broad segments of the population, which is to say, the life of proletarians, as it has always done, as it continues doing by reducing it—since the force relation makes this possible—to the minimum (the minimal services of the neoliberals mean precisely that). At the same time, the neoliberal reorganization of the welfare state operates in reverse. It has transformed the welfare state into an apparatus of assistance to the corporations and the wealthy who increase the inequalities instead of reducing them. The French president Emmanuel Macron defines this logic very well: it is necessary to "aid the wealthy" (so that they produce the wealth that will "trickle down" to the bottom) and "instill responsibility in the poor" (make them feel guilty while impoverishing them).

Similarly, capital does not care in the least about the generalized destruction of the planet's possibilities of life, which are, precisely, the conditions of its accumulation. Capitalism, in two hundred years, has succeeded in destroying what "nature" had taken milleniums to produce. To object that in this way it places itelf in danger, that it needs a planet and it needs labor power is to understand nothing about its "rationality." Pierre Dardot and Christian Laval published a book inspired by Foucault, *La Nouvelle Raison du monde* [*The World's New Reason*], which gives a very sanitized image of neoliberalism (without the South American civil wars) and which analyzes it in terms of its "rationality," whereas "money, money-capital, is a point of dementia that in psychiatry would have only one equivalent: what is called the terminal state [...] Everything is rational in capitalism, except capital or capitalism. A market mechanism that is perfectly rational, on can comprehend it, learn it, and yet it is completely wacko, it is insane."[46]

Fascism and war are always possible because this rationality continually pushes things to the limitless, to the unlimited exploitation of every resource, human and non-human. If it is true, as Marx thought, that capital constantly displaces the limits it has itself created, the 20th century taught us that this displacement cannot occur without wars and without fascist violence. Keynes, a great observer of his fellow citizens, had no illusions about the violence of the response by capitalists ("capable of extinguishing the sun and the stars") to anything threatening profit and property. And the threat also comes from the very irrationality of capital, for, still according to Keynes, "the self-destructive rules of financial calculation govern every aspect of existence."

The Disappearance of Strategic Thinking

> "Before being, there is politics."
> — Gilles Deleuze and Félix Guattari

Without war and without revolution, political movements have lost all strategic knowledge and all sensitivity to the political contingencies, ruptures, turns of events, changes of political phase. This fact is all the more surprising considering that the most original philosophy inspired by '68 is that of the event. But one has the impression that is has been applied to everything, except to the political conflict with capital.

Even if the political framework, the nature of capitalism and of political subjects have radically changed, reconquering a strategic point of view could reinvigorate contemporary movements, which seem guided both by a temporality of the here and now (refusal to defer change to a promised future) and by a long temporality (construction of autonomous and independent forms of life), without regard to any strategic temporality.

Walter Benjamin warns us against abandoning strategic thought by giving a definition of politics that integrates ruptures of history's continuum with an art of revolution's contingency: "History doesn't know the bad infinity contained in the image of two combatants eternally wrestling each other. Genuine politics is calculated in dates when things come due."[47]

Critical thought is not very sensitive to the *kairos*; it has trouble grasping the contingency of political situations. History's turning points seem to elude it. Thus Dardot and Aval, with a timing that was completely off, proposed a reconstruction of the Foucauldian governmentality and its subjugations at the very moment when these were ceasing to function. Problematizing war (and revolution) involves assuming a viewpoint that is irreducible to sociology, to philosophy, to political theory. Such a gesture was accomplished in the first half of the 1970s by Michel Foucault, who introduced "strategy," without great success (the "without great success" concerned Foucault himself). Strategy: "what makes the historical events of humanity or human actions decipherable."[48] The concept and the practice were borrowed directly from the military analysts. Strategy can elucidate "the antagonism that exists when a situation presents itself where enemies clash, a situation where one wins and the other loses," a situation that corresponds perfectly to our actuality, where those who won and those who lost constitute parallel worlds moving away from each other at the speed of the "reforms" that are put into place. But this affirmation remains generic unless we add that, since 1789, strategy has revolution and counter-revolution as its content—it is this idea in fact that underpins the quote from Benjamin given above.

Strategic thought reconfigures the exercise of power by spelling out what we have outlined above. A large part of the feminist movements appears to overlook war and strategy, while integrating and carrying to its extreme consequences the critique of power as *repression* and affirming, on the contrary, its *productive* action. Judith Butler, for example, affirms the non-essentialist nature of sexuality, more *produced* by discourse than *repressed*: "sexuality is saturated with power" or "coextensive with power," hence entirely constructed by it. This is how she interprets the Foucault of volume one of *The History of Sexuality*. But that book authorizes a different reading: thanks to "war," which he makes ample use of *for the last time*, Foucault develops a strategic perspective which, far from making the "productive" and the "repressive" aspects disappear, *subordinates them to strategy*.

Power is defined by a multiplicity of force relations and strategies that are "local and unstable" at once, producing themselves at every moment and coming from everywhere. "[The] multiple force relations that form and operate in the apparatuses of production, in families, in small groups, in the institutions, serve as a support for broad effects of division that run through the whole social body."[49] Power, like sexual domination, is not a thing, an institution, a "law," a structure, but "the name that is lent to a strategic situation."[50] Strictly speaking, it doesn't produce these relations between forces, it limits itself to "coding" them and "integrating" them. By coding and integrating them, it encloses the strategic relations, for a time and never completely, within institutions, norms, and apparatuses [*dispositifs*]. The "never completely" means that sexuality, like the other codifications (economic, political, etc.) is never "saturated with power," is never "coextensive with power."

Quite on the contrary, "power relations [...] are generators of transformation,"[51] so that a situation is always modifiable, because power *relations* are also part of the points of resistance ("in the power relation these play the role of adversary, of target, of support, of projection for a capture"). These "generators of transformation" can be activated when they have the possibility of producing a political rupture and entering into a struggle and a strategy.[52] What poses a problem and was subsequently rejected by Foucault himself, is the *warlike* form of these relations and their strategies.

"This multiplicity of force relations can be coded either in the form of 'war,' or in the form of 'politics'; this would be two different strategies (but quick to morph into one another) for integrating these unbalanced, heterogeneous, unstable, and tense relations of force."[53] Politics (law, the state, the political system) don't replace war; politics and war are always strategies "quick to morph into one another," but *under the hegemony of the machine of capital.* While the two strategies are at the service of power (of capital's machine), they can also be mobilized by revolution. They seem more suited to political activity than simply to performative or discursive action, which can certainly form part of a political strategy, but providing they don't reduce the latter to performance and discourse. Teresa de Lauretis, in an article in which she analyzes, among other things, queer theory's use of the notion of the productiveness of power, cautions against a double danger: first, one mustn't speak of power generically because capital has "gotten in shape and goes to the gym every other day"; secondly and consequently, in political action one cannot understate the domination of capital, which "is always deadly. Foucault notwitstanding."[54]

According to Foucault, there is not "*one* locus of great refusal, soul of revolt, source of all rebellions, pure law of revolution." This has been an acknowledged truth since the 1970s. But it's also established that the multiplicity of force relations, including those inherent in sexuality, can express itself, problematize itself, subjectify itself in a radical way only during revolutionary ruptures. It is precisely there that one manages to get rid of the posture of "governed" and reconnect with confrontation, strategy, and the opening up of possibilities— something that was discovered by the radical wing of the gay movement during the fantastic political ruptures of the fantastic Italian 1970s, struggle as "war"[55] that clearly defined its enemy: "the capitalist heterosexual norm." Combat is not limited to a politics of "recognition" of the diversity of human subjects (Butler), but goes to the root of things. According to a logic that fits squarely in the revolutionary tradition, the capitalist heterosexual norm can only be destroyed; one can free oneself, and free even the boss of his alienation, only by destroying the *power relation of which the boss and the worker are the expression.*

We shall let this conception of the social relation as war function, beyond Foucault, as what still and always makes decipherable the historical events of contemporary capitalism, because the best way to describe our situation is this: a "triumph" of the capitalist forces, a defeat of the anticapitalist critique and practice.

Strategy casts a new light on the operation of capital's "social machine." Defining this machine by production ("mode of production"), by the commodity (an immense accumulation of commodities, even become "images," as with the situationists) or by "structure," "system," or again, defining it exclusively as a "social relationship," is to eliminate one of its constituent elements: class wars and their articulations (race war and sex war), which permeate it and make it exist since the conquest of the Americas.

The conception of capital that I am defending, as a linking of machines and strategies, a series of mechanizations (economic, technological, institutional, etc.) and a political strategy that actualizes them, subjectifies them in a struggle between political adversaries, is in polemical opposition to almost all the contemporary readings of capitalism.

The different theories of '68 thought have granted a primacy to completely contingent phenomena—lines of flight, the working class, resistance: these ontologies described the situation opened up by the period of proletarian revolutions, where the minority constituted by the workers had become a political force, had invented and organized a class dualism, thwarted and often anticipated the movements of capital. That period came to an end immediately after '68. The autonomy and independence of of political movements disappeared at light speed with the exhaustion of revolution and the installation of neoliberalism. The theories of lines of flight, of class, of resistance without "revolution," deprived of the possibility of imposing their own strategy, became impotent.

The decisions and strategies I refer to are not those of a sovereign, but of a multiplicity of forces (capitalists, administrations, military leaders, politicians, etc.) who, as confrontation develops, manage to shape them collectively, through successes and partial failures, in situations that are always contingent. Capitalism did not have a pre-made strategy that it was just a matter of implementing. What it brought to the fore, what constituted the guiding thread of its politics, was instead a class point of view, a class hatred, a hunger for profit and revenge against a revolution that had taken years to configure itself and assert itself.

Consequently, the political defeat was also a theoretical defeat. It seems to be difficult to face that obvious fact; one is content to establish a theoretical continuity with '68 thought without wondering about its failures and its political dead ends. So the rest of this book will focus a critical gaze not just on capital, anti-capitalist struggles, and their respective strategies, but also on the theories and their strategies.

It is not a question of re-examining one of the conquests of '68 thought, the linking together of micropolitics and macropolitics, but of maintaining that the situation has radically changed. The warlike and repressive action of capital clearly reveals itself since 2008 and the blockage of the "real" economy (the financial economy, however, has continued to proliferate), a blockage that cannot be overcome by a simple "creative destruction" à la Shumpeter, but requires a changeover from politics combined with economy to "war" (at present, one just sees beginnings, possibilities of civil war). What is at issue in the rise of the new fascisms is this changeover.

This change of strategy is not self-evident, it involves hesitations, a battle within the elites, but, for the moment, if capital's war machine is to stay on course in the deepening of neoliberalism and political secession, it has no other possibilities. Codification and capture on the part of capital are always temporary and partial because they depend on the strategies. It is always possible to reverse the situation, provided power relations are considered from the strategic point of view.

Critical thinking, like anticapitalist movements, arrives at this political turning point completely unprepared, having been unable to anticipate the evolution of capital with its "outgrowths of power" which the neofascisms constitute. The limits of post-'68 political theories don't just concern the nature and definition of capitalism, but first of all the "war machine" that one wishes to set against it. The political and theoretical failure resides in the inability to go beyond the experience of Leninism, since the criticisms in regard to it, while fully justified, have never given rise to an organization that could mount a defense and an attack, and that would be remotely comparable to the war machine it constructed.

2

Technical Machine and War Machine

"It's a fact that we always let ourselves be bam-
boozled by the possibilities [...] No one worries
about the actual results. One simply sticks with
the possibilities. The actual results of radio are
deplorable, but its possibilities are 'infinite,' so
radio is a good thing. It is a very bad thing."
— Bertolt Brecht

In the 1920s, the social-democrat Kautsky was
convinced of the premodern nature of fascism:
because it was born in an Italy that was still largely
agricultural, it couldn't install itself in a modern
industrial nation like Germany. Historical fascism
was a vestige of the past, an archaism such that
once the parenthesis of the dictatorship had been
closed, the progress of the productive forces would
erase it forever. Nothing could be more false: historical fascism was just as modern as capitalism, it
was even one of capitalism's expressions, as Italian
futurism clearly shows.

The same is true of the new fascism, which is a *cyberfascism*. It invalidates all the utopias—from cyberpunk to cyberfeminism, from the cyber-sphere to cyberculture—which, since the post-war period and with an intensification starting in the 1970s, sees in cybernetic machines the promise of a new post-human subjectivity and an emancipation from capitalist domination. Bolsonaro and Trump have utilized all the available technologies of digital communication, but their victory doesn't come from technology; it results from a political machine and a strategy that links a micropolitics of sad affects (frustration, hatred, envy, anxiety, fear) to the macropolitics of a new fascism that gives political consistency to the subjectivities devastated in the financialization.

To say it in the terms that will be employed in this chapter, the technical machine, in all its forms, is brought into the service of the strategy put in place by the neofascist social machine, which, under the conditions of capitalism, can only be a war machine. This banal observation collides with a conception whereby technics, like any other juridical or eco-nomic apparatus, would incorporate power relations by pacifying and depersonalizing them. The power of the technical apparatus, exercised by automatic operations, would be normalized to a point where it would be difficult "to detect a violence" in the process, to repeat the words of Negri and Hardt.

Such statements, as old as liberalism, seem to find a new confirmation in cybernetics and the new technologies that are thought to possess, like the "market," a self-regulating and self-correcting capacity. In this way, the automatic and impersonal functioning of social norms would be reinforced by the automatic and impersonal operations of technics. "Nothing, absolutely nothing can resist automatization," declares even Catherine Malabou. Citing Bourdieu, she adds that "the state doesn't necessarily need to give orders and apply a *physical coercion*, or a *disciplinary constraint*, in order to produce an organized social world." It suffices for it to have "bodies habituated" by automatic operations.[1]

This depoliticized conception of apparatuses that self-automate and acquire an impersonal life of their own has its roots in Marxism (commodity fetishism) as well as in liberalism (the invisible hand of the market). In the 20th century, German philosophy further radicalized the power that apparatuses have over the people who produced them, identifying them with a technology whose development was experiencing un unprecedented advancement. Heidegger makes this the last figure of metaphysics, while Günther Anders, who does give it a more political reading, makes capital disappear into the "autonomous" operation of machines.

In this way, there emerges an alternative between those who attribute to the technical machine the power of destruction and subjugation which is actually that of the machine of capital, and those for whom the power exercised by the machine is assimilable to the power described by Foucault (it entices, solicits, encourages, makes certain actions possible and others impossible—action upon another action is its modus operandi, which replaces "physical coercion" or "disciplinary constraint"). What is blanked out in all these cases is the relation between strategy, social machine, and technical machine.

We are going to problematize precisely what these theories repress. The depersonalization of power relations which technics carries out (automation) exalts the partisan point of view, favors strategic choice, and centralizes decision-making instead of making it disappear into the anonymity of operation (system, structure, etc.). So that it is in fact the war machine that takes precedence over the technical machine. In this sense, technology is one of the major stakes in the war within the population.

The coming of the new fascisms offers an additional confirmation of the fact that, in capitalism, the political order, maintained by economic, juridical, and technological apparatuses, is continually disrupted, not by technical innovations, but by revolutions and counter-revolutions. It is war machines that cause these ruptures, by orienting, actualizing, giving consistency to the "apparatuses" (including the technological ones), and not the reverse.

The rupture constituted by the new fascisms did not come from outside capitalism, as a result of crises; in reality, fascism is lodged very deeply in the organization of labor ("abstract" and indifferent to all use value, "labor" can function in the same way in the production of cars and the production of mass extermination) and the organization of consumption (abstract and "indifferent" to all the modalities of its production, including to child labor or the servile labor of millions of workers in the world's "great South"). Because they have forgotten these truths, critical analysts have trouble grasping the contours of these new fascisms, which they most often define as populisms and authoritarianisms.

Social Machine or War Machine

According to cybernetic theories, cognitive capitalism, or accelerationism, contemporary society, compared to those preceding it, would have the particularity of being invaded, shaped and governed by machines. However, in his day, Lewis Mumford had already changed the terms of the debate, by arguing that every society is itself a machine or, better still, a "megamachine," an idea that inspired Deleuze and Guattari to develop their concept of "social machine." In *The Myth of the Machine*,[2] he shows that it is society as megamachine that engenders, assembles, and organizes men and technical machines in the same process. For example, the archaic Egyptian megamachine of the Pharoahs was composed, on the one hand, of a multitude of human elements, the slaves—"specialized, interchangeable," "rigorously marshalled together and coordinated in a process centrally organized and centrally directed"[3].... and, on the other hand, of very simple technical machines—the inclined plane and the level (the wheel, the pulley, the screw had not yet been invented). As it evolves, this megamachine is replacing "humans" by technical machines. But the latter will never be able to replace the megamachine; the technical machines will never be able to self-automate and dominate the social machine.

Numerous material, semiotic, imaginary, cosmic, and subjective elements distinguish the megamachine from the technical machine. The megamachine is composed of humans—whose "mechanization" predated by far that of their tools, the "simple machines of classical mechanics" —and of signs ("translating speech into graphic record not only made it possible to transmit impulses and messages throughout the system, but to fix accountability when writtens orders were not carried out").[4] The megamachine required many more elements to be able to create the men/machines assemblage and make it function: the royalty myth of divine right, sun worship and the "cosmic fantasies," which alone can guarantee the transformation of "men into mechanical objects and the assembling of these objects into a machine."[5] In addition, the functioning of the megamachine demanded an enslavement ensured by "techniques" that would train the slaves in submission, on the one hand, and, on the other, the priests and bureaucracy of command. The "workers had minds of a new order, executing each task in strict obedience to instructions, infinitely patient, limiting their response to the word of command."[6] As for the subjectivities of the "caste of priests and of the bureaucracy," they guaranteed, respectively, "a reliable organization of knowledge, natural and supernatural" and "an elaborate structure for giving orders, carrying them out, and following them through."[7] The enormous productivity of this machine having very rudimentary technologies at its disposal, is primarily that of the social machine. If this is obvious with regard to the Egypt of the pharaohs, it is still true of a social machine liked ours, equipped with much more sophisticated technologies.

Now that we have introduced the concept of the social machine (or megamachine), let's try to move on to another stage. To the concept of social machine, I prefer another concept of Deleuze and Guattari's, that of "war machine," which I will redirect somewhat. Foucault did an excellent job of showing how it was necessary to rid oneself of "sociologism," by which he meant the tendency of the social sciences to cover power relations under the action of all-encompassing, generic, holistic entities, such as Society, the Social, and social relations. The problem is that the anonymity of "society" and its mechanisms masks relations of war, class divisions, and various dominations. Power must be analyzed on the basis of its own strategies, which are always singular, event-driven, and unpredictable, following no other regularity than that of their affirmation. Consequently, I will abandon the generic and imprecise notion of "social machine," which seems to produce, in an impersonal manner, norms, dispositions [*habitus*], and laws, in favor of "war machine," which implies the dominant and the dominated, relations between forces on the basis of which norms, dispositions and laws are produced, but also a certain amount of "causing-to-die" and violence, exactly as in the Egyptian megamachine. When sociology pushes its analysis so far as to include domination (Bourdieu), it describes the mechanisms on which this domination depends, but it neglects the will to resist and revolt, the possibility to form oneself into a revolutionary machine against the existing powers, which involves the concept of war. "War machine" signifies therefore, at variance with Deleuze and Guattari, that society is divided, that there are opposing forces and those forces manifest themselves through strategies of confrontation, including through technology. It is precisely this distinction between technical machine and war machine that is missing from the concept of machine deployed by Günther Anders. Drawing from his experience as an assembly line worker in a large American factory during his exile, he tranforms Heidegger's famous formula, according to which man is "the shepherd of being," by saying "the shepherd of machines," a gesture that seems to open up more perspectives. But this is what he explains: "Since the *raison d'être* of machines resides in performance, and even in maximum performance, they need *environments* that guarantee this maximum. And they conquer what they need. Every machine is expansionist, not to say imperialist; each one creates its own *colonial empire* of services (comprising transporters, operational teams, consumers). [...] The original machine grows, therefore, becoming a "megamachine" [...] it also requires an exterior world, a "colonial empire" that submits to it and does its bidding. [...] No limit is placed on self-expansion; *the machines' thirst for accumulation is unquenchable.*"[8] Continuing its expansion, it becomes a "global machine," a "total machine" that succeeds in fully conquering the world. The "world becomes a machine," a techno-totalitarian State, constituted by a "gigantic machine park."

However, as we've just seen, Mumford's "mega-machine" has nothing mechanical about it. On the contrary, it is the site of conflicts, decisions, and strategies—it is a war machine, in fact. It's easy to understand that everywhere Anders writes "machine," we should read "capital": it is not the technical machine that has this "thirst for accumulation," but the war machine of capital. The gap between the "power of production," which constantly increases, and the ability to "grasp" it, which is, according to Anders, at the root of present-day man's powerlessness, can only be filled by a different war machine, a revolutionary one.

The war machine doesn't just produce the technical machine, but also the humans that serve it. Our analysis will be deployed in reference to three strategies and three ways of articulating the arrangement [*agencement*] between humans and non-humans: Trump's supremacist machine, the revolutionary machine of the Algerian FLN, and the machine of the Second World War.

The Supremacist War Machine

In the USA, the government of behaviors appeared to have been integrated with the development of the new technologies, configuring in this way the "future" exercise of the power described by all the "cyber" theories. But Trump and his war machine decided such matters differently, by conjuring up that which tehnology was supposed to stave off with its pious habits, the "specters of civil war," the "violence that founds" neoliberalism.

The great American corporations that are at the leading edge of technological innovation (the GAFAM: Google, Amazon, Facebook, Apple, Microsoft) produce the subjectivity and "relation to oneself" needed for the functioning of their apparatuses and for guiding the behavior of the governed in general. This governmentality integrated with the technical machines would have the power to anticipate and control behaviors, framing the future (the possible and excluded human actions) in advance, by profiling individuals based on digital "traces" of their performances and calculated by the algorithms of superpowerful computers. These machines seem to embody a *pacification of power relations*, since, thanks to them, power would be exercised in a depersonalized manner.

The GAFAM promote a *smart* figure of "human capital," that lives in a *smart* city, eats *smart*, and communicates *smart*, a subjectivity open to sexual and cultural differences as well as to the market. These companies, supplying the imaginary, the values, and the contents of contemporary capitalism and the models of its actualization, penetrate into the most intimate areas of everyday life, occupying subjectivities and their affects 24/7. By constantly soliciting one's attention—giving rise to an activity as absurd as compulsively consulting one's smartphone —they produce the apparatuses of the contemporary General Mobilization. They tirelessly fabricate an information designed to affect subjectivities, circulating through billions of telephones, televisions, computers, tablets, whose connections envelop the planet in a thicker and thicker net. They convey an uninterrupted flow of advertising displaying the same model of *smart* living for *smart* families.

The most depoliticized of the "cyber" critics assert that under these conditions all political action is impossible: the information is too rapid, too intense, too dense, and too complex for individuals and collectives to address politically. Political action presupposes a deliberate and collectively shared treatment of information which its digital circulation rules out.

And yet every day, in this "chaos" of information, the corporate boards, the big banks, the States, the mafias easily manage to select, elaborate, and extract strategies, political moves, and profits. The complexity, the overabundance of information, images, and discourses constitute a serious problem for an individual submerged by these flows, but not for a social machine capable of selecting and elaborating them collectively (a collective composed of humans and non-humans). The war machine assembled by Trump orients itself, chooses, and decides in this jumble. The problem is political before being technological.

The Silicon Valley firms contributed largely to creating the situation that allowed Trump to take power. The dizzying succession of technological "revolutions" (digital programs, platforms, smart cities, smartphones, bitcoins, bio- and nano-technologies, artificial intelligence, etc.) produced the most immobile of social immobilities while the dissemination of these technologies strongly reinforced power relations instead of unsettling them.These firms are the very example of the power of monopolies (hence of unearned income) and symbols of the concentration of property (they currently post the highest market capitalizations) pursued by every means, not the least of which is tax evasion. The horizontal distribution of power promised by the miniaturization of computers resulted in its opposite, monopolies that have far outstripped those of the industrial age.

The acceleration of innovation, made possible by an exponential increase in calculating power, led straight to a hyper-technological "*ancien régime*" where the positions to be occupied in the hierarchy of jobs, incomes, assets, education, living spaces, etc. depend on birth, exactly as they did before the French Revolution. Thus, from the transhumanism of Silicon Valley there emerges not a "post-human" self, but a very familiar figure, the aristocrat, having become *cyber* and with a head, cut off in 1789, that has grown back. Confidence in technology as a means of creating more liberty, more democracy, and less enslavement is belied once more by the truly deplorable "actual results" of this reproduction of power relations.

Trump is a new type of fascist and racist that can be called a "cyborg": his "consistency" is inseparable from the technical machines (television, internet, Twitter) with and by which he exists as a "political subject." Similarly, his electors "exist" and manifest themselves politically by those same cyber-apparatuses. But his hybridization with the machine is not what makes him a new fascist "self." It is his political strategy and his subjectification that give a new configuration and new functions to the cybernetic setup. He was not the candidate either of the classic media system or the great Silicon Valley corporations that control the "social networks." He won because he was able to express and politically construct neofascist, racist, and sexist subjectivities, basing himself on the social and psychic devatastation produced by financialization and digitalization. He gave "voice" and political expression to the fears and anxieties of the indebted, fueled and amplified by the media, by shifting confrontation onto the identitarian terrain, by playing a part of the population (White men) off against the others (migrants, women, foreigners, and all the minorities). He captured subjectivities crushed by forty years of economic policies that systematically impoverished them and by media policies that scorned them as "fogeys" resistant to any modernization and rejecting any reform. Throughout the so-called "public debt crisis," the news commentary accompanying the strategy for saving the banking system called upon the registers of "order" ("The debt has to be paid"), "threat" ("If you don't pay it, the system will break down, and you along with it," and "insult" ("It's your fault! People like you are lazy!").[9] Order, threat, and insult: these are the characteristics of the media which Trump appropriated in his use of the same media, turning them back against the elites who divided up the democratic governmentality amongst themselves.

The power of the *smart* words and images of GAFAM and the media networks was neutralized, because it was confronted by a different war machine, capable of constructing a politics with its supremacist, racist, and sexist slogans. Their information bounced off the surface of the neofascist "self" and didn't affect it in the least (the governed, whose characteristic is to "respond to the solicitations" of the governmental apparatuses, refused to play the game, thus escaping their control). The technological "automatisms" are completely ineffective in a situation of open conflict in which everyone chooses their camp and becomes an "informational partisan." The big digital firms weren't able to construct the consensual reality of democratic public opinion, since the neoliberal governmentality was rejected in advance and this refusal found a social machine to carry it and give it substance. The affects conveyed by the "sensitive" omnipotence of Silicon Valley can't do anything against the affects (fear, frustration, anxiety, desire for revenge) amplified and organized by the media war machine of "resentment" called Trump. The predictive and anticipatory capacity that billions and billions of data should ensure turned out to be deficient. Data can predict when I will eat a margherita pizza, if I eat one often, but predicting a political rupture is logically impossible, even for an infinite network of computers. Data can govern the behaviors of those who accept what "is," but they can't predict or "govern" the behaviors of subjectivities in revolt.

The oh-so futuristic Silicon Valley folded, therefore, faced with the emergence of the "new archaisms." What reveals the political weakness of these companies regarded as the models of the economy and the power of the future is the rupturing operation organized by the extreme right: it unleashed a political battle within the capitalist elites that will probably end with their recomposition around an accentuation of the neoliberal policies which only the neofascist organizations can successfully complete. One shouldn't underestimate what has happened in Europe and the United States, because this reactionary wave will continue to spread (in Brazil, once more, the autonomy of technics has lasted, integrated without difficulty with a fascist political strategy). With the international sequence of 2011, Brazil in 2013, and Greece in 2015, the intensification of the debt crisis had made visible the emergence of a conflictual subjectification on a world scale and the possibility of a political rupture. In spite of the weakness of those political movements, part of the capitalist elites preferred to play the card of the neofascisms, racism, sexism, xenophobia. Racism thus became the main mode of strategic management of the war against the populations, divided according to nationality or origin, as concerns citizenship and the labor market.

What is to be questioned, therefore, is not the omnipotence but the impotence of these giant firms, their machines and their algorithms that are meant to govern us, because they never manage to penetrate into the territories and networks that politically assert their independence and their political autonomy. These technical machines are very effective when it comes to isolated, desolidarized, fear-ridden individuals, subjected to capitalist processing and placed in relation solely by the apparatuses of media democracy. But, confronted by a socialization, a taking of sides, and collective expressions of rupture, fascist or not, they suddenly become powerless.

Instead of celebrating the power of the GAFAM, a clear sign of our powerlessness, we should begin to regard them as the 19th century revolutionaries regarded other war machines—that is, as "paper tigers" whose weakness is not technical but political. Useless, then, to try and compete on their terrain, a losing proposition. It is not technical machines that install knowledges, powers, and their automatisms, it is war machines. Félix Guattari, to whom we owe the concept, points out that steam-powered machines were invented in China, where they were utilized as innocent games for children. The war machine is what determines the use of the steam engine. The war machine can just as well make an infernal instrument of it, as in the factories of the 19th century, or, mounted onto a locomotive, the very image of progress.

What is essential is to construct a revolutionary war machine. On that basis, one can develop a technological machine, whereas the opposite is not possible. Only forty years after the revolution, the Soviets, who had gone through a terrible civil war, then an even more dreadful war against the Nazis, sent the first man into space, ahead of the American superpower. At the time of the revolution, China was the poorest country in the world. Today, it rivals the giants of Silicon Valley and the economic might of the USA. Although the extraordinary subjective strength developed by the war machine was invested in, diverted into, neocapitalist and neo-authoritarian projects, its potential remains. Science, technology, and expertise can be imported and even copied, as post-war Japan did. Lewis Mumford had already noted that "All the properties of particular machines—masive energy use, mechanization, automation, quantitative yield—were accrued thanks to their inclusion in the megamachine," the social machine.

The first step toward understanding and utilizing technical machines is political in nature. But the different post-'68 political movements did not manage to problematize or even imagine a new war machine. The greatest victory of neoliberalism, registered deep in the "collective brain" (General Intellect) was the erasure of that which characterized the last century: the long sequence of successful or failed revolutions.

Fanon and Radio

We don't lack critical viewpoints concerning technical machines, but a theory of their relationship with the revolutionary machine. The most surprising text for trying to articulate this relationship was written by Franz Fanon and has to do with the function of the technical apparatus called "radio" during the colonial war and the struggle for Algeria's national independence. "This is the voice of Algeria,"[10] the second chapter of *L'an V de la révolution algérienne*, brings out in an incomparable way the force of the war machine that actualizes the possibilities of the technical machine in a revolutionary sense.

Radio was an integral part of the power strategies of the French colonizer and it contributed to the processes of subjugation to which the colonized were subjected. But what interests us here is the radical change of "attitudes," the colonized's way of perceiving and feeling, and their "behaviors" in relation to the technical apparatus, the world, and themselves, when the war machine of the national revolution deployed its force. Fanon shows that the appearance of a "technological apparatus," its penetration, its dissemination, its acceptability or its rejection always depended on a war machine.

The reception or rejection of newscasts, the possibility of selecting the contents and critiquing them or, on the contrary, undergoing their power, depends on the presence or absence of a "social body." Rejection or acceptance are not simply competencies, faculties, capacities of the individual; they are "socially" and politically constituted. The technical instrument is "never perceived in itself, in a calm neutrality." It is always situated within a political political strategy and, in the case of Algeria, it intervened in the colonial situation where the differences, the hostilities, the "negative or positive factors always exist in a very emphatic way."

In the colony, "the social dichotomy reaches an extraordinary intensity," so that the voice of the radio is not "undifferentiated," "neutral," but is the "voice of the oppressor, the voice of the enemy." This pushing of concepts to the limit contains more truth about the media than that expressed by press "freedom" in a pacified democracy. "All the French speech that was heard was an order, a threat, or an insult." The fact that broadcast information was "order, threat, and insult" is far from constituting a colonial exception. On the contrary, these are chracteristics of such information in general.

In Algeria, radio and its "sensory and intellectual powers" were the object of a refusal that was passive at first: "The speech delivered was not received, deciphered, understood, but rejected [...] the communication was simply refused." "Before the rebellion, there was the truth of the colonizer and the nullity of the colonized," a situation that breeds distrust, refusal, and rejection, but without there being a collective response, constitutive of a war machine. "There was no organized resistance." The rejection of the radio and its broadcasts was not the expression of "an explicit, organized, and grounded resistance."

The war machine produces non-human apparatuses, and it models and modulates humans down to their "interiority." The voice of the colonizer, "the voice of Frenchmen speaking to Frenchmen," intervened in the micropolitical dimension, for example by clashing with the traditional family structure. The "undifferentiated" programs were not suited to the patriarchal hierarchization of the Algerian family. Impossible to listen to the radio programs together, because they endangered the traditional sociability of the "feudal" family relations: "The sex allusions or even the clownish situations caused an unendurable strain. The effects and affects of the radio were even more pronounced from a psychopathological standpoint." Before 1954, the monographs written on Algerians suffering from hallucinations constantly pointed out the presence in the 'external action phase' of highly aggressive and hostile radio voices. These metallic, cutting, insulting, disagreeable voices all had for the Algerian an accusing, inquisitorial character." In the psychopathological domain, the radio was "an evil object, anxiogenic and accursed."

A "veritable mutation" occurred in 1956, with the advent of the radio programs of the liberation army ("The Voice of Free Algeria"). This revolutionary event created new possibilities that primarily affected subjectivity and began its transformation. "Contesting the very principle of foreign domination leads to essential mutations in the consciousness of the colonized, in the perception he has of the colonizer, in his situation of a man in the world." Mutations that didn't just stop with the "political" dimension, but went on to affect the micropolitical dimension through the fabrication of unconscious elements. The actualization of the new possibilities created by the rupture was the task of the revolutionary machine which, by establishing a new relationship between the radio (technical machine) and its listeners (subjectivity), undermined the colonialist functioning of the same technology.

The difference in technological capacity between the political adversaries was enormous, but the problem was not there: that gap was encountered in all conflicts and revolutionary wars, which are assymetric by definition. In the 19th and especially in the 20th century, in Russia, in China, in Vietnam, in Africa, or in South America, the military machine and the communication machine of imperialism, although equipped with all the latest technologies and inventions, were considered as defeatable. The revolutionary machine revealed and analyzed the enemy's power of military weaponry and hyper-tehnological organization, but also his powerlessness, his weaknesses, his political flaws.

In the revolutionary war, the colonized became an active subject, even if he or she didn't participate directly in the political organization, because the radio included them in "a community on the move" for which they would feel like an "actor." The "extremely technicized French services" systematically jammed the transmissions of the FLN radio, seriously interfering with their programs. Thus, the battle was also waged on the terrain of the radio waves ("the war of the waves") and the colonized learned how to select and develop information from a strategic point of view, by choosing their camp, by becoming an information partisan. "The listener was incorporated into the battle of the radio waves, figuring out the enemy's tactics, and in an almost physical way, foiling his strategy."

The colonizing army's jamming made the "voice choppy, discontinuous [...] often inaudible." It obliged the listener to perform "a veritable work of elaboration," of interpretation, decoding, and imagination. He "compensated for the fragmentary nature of the news with an autonomous creation of imagination." Behind the crackling, the listener made out not only the voice of the revolution, but also the battles against the occupier. The information was minimal, almost nonexistent, but this void was filled with the power of the ongoing revolutionary action. The revolution transformed the passive refusal into an active attitude that completed the fragmentary news "with an autonomous creation of imagination." Under these conditions, saying one had heard the Voice of Algeria was a lie—the sabotage of the airwaves by the French iwas effective. But this meant "making a deliberate choice between the enemy's congential lie and the people's own lie, which acquired a dimension of truth."

The reception of information was no longer individual, it no longer took place in isolation and fear, but within a "community," a "social body" in which the listener was an active participant. "The truth of the oppressor that used to be rejected as an absolute lie was finally opposed by an active truth." In order to become an information "partisan," there has to be a political rupture and a political machine that divides not only the information, but first of all the society.

The event of revolution had also opened up the possibility of a transformation of patriarchal relations in the family. From the micropolitical viewpoint, the subjective mutation of the Algerians made possible what was previously impossible, listening together, as a family, the scrambled broadcasts of the revolutionary radio which broke down the old patriarchal hierarchies: one could see "fathers, mothers, and daughters listening to the news together." Fanon even observes a radical change from the psychological point of view. In the hallucinatory psychoses, "the radio voices became protective, friendly. Insults and accusations disappeared and gave way to words of encouragement" Fanon knew, without waiting for the theorists to tell him, that the infosphere constituted a psycopathogenic environment. But contrary to the depoliticization which they ensure, he attributes many of these pathologies to colonialism's war machine and works toward the construction of a revolutionary war machine, to which he assigns the task, if not of treating them, at least of modifying the environment so that it is more favorable to a positive progression of the psyche. The "foreign" technique, the technique of power, "digested" and appropriated "on the occasion of the national struggle, became an instrument of combat for the people and a protective organ against anxiety." "Every Algerian felt called upon and wanted to become an element of the vast network of meanings born of the liberating combat."

The appropriation of the "means of production," including radio, is always the achievement of the "social body," never of the individual body. It can only occur through political action. It is the political community in motion that takes possession of the technical machine in order to transform it. "As a mental process, starting in 1956 one witnessed *virtually an invention of the radio technique*." In reality, an invention of the war machine, which engendered both a "new technique" and a "new subjectivity." Finally, then, Brecht could have said that radio is not just a possibility, but also a good thing.

Cybernetics and War

"The media system proceeded in three phases. Phase 1, starting with the American Civil War, developed techniques of storage for sound, image, and writing: film, the gramophone, and the man-machine system that is the typewriter. Phase 2, starting with the First World War, developed for the stored contents appropriate electrical techniques of transmission: radio, television [...] Phase 3, since the Second World War, converted the functional schema of the typewrtiter into a technique of prediction. The mathematical definition of calculability, 'computability,' given by Turing in 1936, gave its name to the future computers."

— Friedrich Kittler

Cybernetics is the direct result of the action upon science and technology of the State machine at war. War functions here as a productive force capable of accelerating the emplacement of the technological invention and of a new type of scientist. Strategy and war are not realities foreign to cybernetic technology and big science which would be added on from outside their normal operation. On the contrary, they have been the breeding ground of these entities. Cybernetics and big science were conceived, tried out, and utilized during and for the total wars.

Their development, during and after the Second World War was the work of the U.S. Army, the greatest, richest, and most innovative entrepreneur that capitalism has ever known. The power of this *state entrepreneur* is far beyond that of the Shumpeterian captain of industry of the 19th century whose disappearance is regretted. The expression "creative destruction" is almost perfectly applicable to it, provided one reverses its terms, as it were, since here the creation has destruction as its objective. The U.S. Army contains in itself the reversibility of destruction and creation, of economy and war, of acting on an action and of violence upon persons and things, those dualities that constitute contemporary power.

The war machine is not just an external condition of the first cybernetics, since the *enemy* structures it from within. According to Peter Galison, the man/machine hybridization, which presided over the construction of an antiaircraft defense device being tried out for the first time, was conceptualized by Norbert Wiener, the father of cybernetics, based on an image of the enemy he had in his mind. His particular enemy was not the one embodied by the Japanese soldier, in whom the Americans and the British saw "the monstrous alien, radically different and sub-human"; nor was it the "anonymous enemy" that could represent the pilot bombing the cities from the heights of his airplane. The enemy that interested Wiener was "more active" than the anonymous enemy and more "rational" than the racial enemy: "a mechanized and emotionless enemy, capable of predictable movements that could at least be modeled through a kind of '*black box machinery.*' This image of the enemy is less familiar but more powerful than the first two images."[11]

Cybernetics originated in this conception of the enemy. For the radar operator, the pilot of the airplane to be brought down was so well-integrated with the machine that the difference between the human and the non-human tended to disappear. The one assigned to fire the antiaircraft machine gun was caught in a similar hybridization. It was on the basis of this double hybridization that a machine was built which was equipped with feedback and was capable of anticipating the motions of the targeted aircraft.

During the Second World War, the army and the American state laid the foundations of what the Italian Marxists would call the "General Intellect," borrowing the expression from Marx's *Grundrisse*. Making capitalist production less dependent on the labor time of the worker than on the development of science, technology, and communication was the goal pursued through the installation of the great laboratories in which different scientific disciplines and functions are merged. This process was set in motion during the first total war, which required a direct control by the state and capital over scientific production. Research moved outside the university "to tackle organizational problems imposed by the military-industrial structure [...]. For the first time in the history of Europe the technical-military application of science [...] compels the state to have a direct command of research." The management necessary for the manufacture of the atomic bomb required an even more extensive control over scientific production on the part of the state.

In order to develop new technical machines of destruction, the machinery of the warring state models and modulates a new type of researcher and organizes new modalities of productive collaboration that will be perfected and amplified during the Cold War. "The radars or other atomic arms were not conceived by do-it-yourselfers: these technologies took shape during meetings of inter-disciplinary teams made up of scientists, engineers, and managers."[13] The organizational methods that Boltanski and Chapello attribute to the inventiveness of the capitalists after '68 or that the theoreticians of cognitive capitalism see emerging from labor power and the collaboration of cognitive workers were devised by the U.S. Army.

"Though they were hosted and financed by a ponderous bureaucracy, these teams didn't operate according to status and rank, they worked, rather, within a social structure without any real hierarchy. That structure had been created due to the need for a general systemic approach to developing arms, a structure able to envisage men and machines as the paired elements of an unparalleled combat apparatus."[14] Violating the disciplinary and professional boundaries is even the secret of the method. "The pressures brought to bear to produce new technologies of warfare led erstwhile specialists to cross the boundaries of their profession, to mix work and pleasure and to form new interdisciplinary networks within which they would work and live."[15] Wiener emphasizes that this organization integrating work and life, work and pleasure (other characteristics attributed to post-'68 management) was something the scientific community had always dreamed of and the war had brought about. "We agreed about these questions long before we were able to designate the common field of our investigations […] The war determined its nature in our stead."[16]

During the war, another basic change emerged from the teamwork between scientists and this enterprise under the control and supervision of the state/army: the transformation of the figure of the scientist into an entrepreneur. In the war effort, "scientists and engineers learned to act like a company head." This strategy would later be transmitted by the state to the private sector, which would only be a matter of improving it.

What Marx had not foreseen, and what the Marxists of the General Intellect still don't see, is that the development of science, technology, and communication/information has both destruction and production as its end. Technology and science are just components of the war machine that always combines, and irreversibly so from the beginning of the 20th century, capital and war, production and destruction. While this non-hierarchical collaboration between military figures, scientists and engineers was pursued in a relaxed and convivial atmosphere, the American army, thanks to the fruits of this teamwork, massacred people in Corea, in Vietnam, organized the assassination of Allende, and tens of thousands of

South American militants were massacred during the ten years of civil war, under the direction of the war criminal Henry Kissinger.

The hybridization between civil and military did not cease with the end of the total wars. On the contrary, it was intensified during the Cold War with the institutionalization of the military, industrial, and university complex. Even the artists (the avant-garde of the 1950s and 1960s) were involved in this research that upended the methods of organization. The "knowledge society," that was said to be the new horizon of emancipation, was largely anticipated by the American army: for it, science and theoretical knowledge were the powerful impetus for an industrial production dedicated to "destruction."

Neoliberal politics would use all this knowledge, experimentation, and methodological innovation kindly placed at their disposal by the army, and set that to work in the private economy. Once they were cleared of their "military or even governmental filiation, [they] appeared in everyone's eyes as cultural and economic drivers [...] as forces emanating from nature."[17] It was then that the storytelling began of the innovative and genial entrepreneur, confident in the market and distrustful of anything resembling state intervention, capable of taking risks and of inventing the portable computer in his garage. A "cosmic scam" that is sold to us as a truth because the winners had the power to impose it. Silicon Valley is the fruit, not of the spirit of initiative of entrepreneurs finally liberated from bureaucratic tutelage, but of fifty years of huge public investments managed by the most hierarchized, disciplinary, murderous structure that has ever existed, the American army.

The scientists who created and promoted the cybernetic and informational technologies were not naïve. They were perfectly aware that their research strictly depended on the war machine and military financing. In 1950, Wiener predicted that the new cybernetic machines would become implanted in ten to twenty years, unless "violent political changes or another great war"[18] accelerated the process.

Here we have another example of the fact that it is not the great technological tendencies, the productive determinisms, the "objective" development of productive forces, but the political ruptures, the subjective bifurcations of history, the strategic confrontations that introduce remarkable innovations and determine sudden accelerations. In the case that concerns us, it was the urgency of "the Battle of Britain that made it necessary to thoroughly address the problem of radar, by speeding up the natural development of this question that could have taken decades." Owing to the necessities of war, it took only two years to "utilize radar effectively on the battlefield."[19]

Theory of Machines

> "A technical element remains abstract, completely indeterminate, so long as it is not related to an assemblage that it presupposes. What is primary in relation to the technical element is the machine: not the technical machine, but the social or collective machine, the machinic assemblage that will determine what the technical element is at each moment, what its uses are, its extension, its comprehension. It is through the intermediary of the assemblages that the phylum selects, qualifies, and even invents the technical elements."
>
> — Gilles Deleuze and Félix Guattari

The authors who, in the years 1960–1970, profoundly renewed the machine concept have supplied us with a conceptual toolbox for escaping the trap of the "technological revolutions." Extremely sophisticated theories about machines proliferate, always questioning the latest technical machine (algorithms, bitcoins, nanotechnologies, digital platforms, etc.) but never the (capitalist) war machine that selects them and makes them function. So they endlessly repeat the same mistake. The accelerationists, for example, display this naivety when, in their analyses of the operation of finance capital, they conceal the war machine that imposes the creditor/debtor relationship, its strategies ("creditors first") and its subjugations (the indebted individual) behind the impersonal and automatic action of the technique (high-frequency trading) and the algorithms, the mathematical models that make them work.

Accelerationism belongs to that vast and colorful collection of theories which, when they aren't fascinated by technology's progressive potentials, are fascinated by the catastrophe which they seem to announce (Mark Fisher, Franco Berardi, Nick Land, etc.). These two seemingly opposed viewpoints meet in the centrality ascribed to automation and the automatisms: power relations between persons would disappear under the impersonal operation of the machines. "We are governed by algorithms," digital machines conduct our "conducts," "numbers dictate our behaviors," and so on. Franco "Bifo" Berardi, a regular participant in the debates that run through these networks, synthesizes this convergence thusly: "The financial abstraction is based on the impersonal operation of automatisms. No one is making decisions because a logical-mathematical chain has replaced all decision making and the algorithms of capital have become independent of the individual will of those who created them and those who utilize them."

The origin of this depoliticization must be sought in the last spasms of '68 thought, in Lyotard or Baudrillard, for example. In the former, capital is a system with no real outside and consequently has no need of any strategy. Lytoard reduces it to "a factual process," a technological, cybernetic operativity whose only goal is development and whose "only known rule [...] is the maximization of the system's performances."[20] There is no possibility of escaping the operation of the machine. Even "emancipation" is no longer a battle that can be won: "it is now dependent on the system itself" and "the critiques, of whatever nature, are demanded by it with a view to fulfilling this responsibility more effectively."[21] The "dysfunctions" of the system itself are turned back into incentives to increase its performativity. The system can recycle everything, even war, which is only a result, a necessary or contingent accident. This post-sixty-eight version of the "end of history" was soon confronted by its inanity, because the war that wouldn't need to take place (Baudrillard) was not only quite real, but it consisted in the double defeat which the Americans sustained in Iraq and Afghanistan. The digital technology omnipotence that is found at the core of these theories was countered by a simple political strategy—which goes to show that the "real" has not disappeared into a simulation subject to the manipulations of the system. We don't know of any more catastrophically real consequences, for the entire planet, than those of this war concerning which, according to another version of Baudrillard's, it "made absolutely no difference whether it took place or not." Contingency, rupture, the "real" (which cannot be anticipated even with an infinite network of computers) easily make light of these theories which, at the end of their evolution, liquidate revolution and make technology into an autonomous, self-referential power, dependent on no other strategy than that of its own development.

We find the same problem here as in the preceding chapter: the illusion that power relations are completely immanent, here to technology, there to law and the economy. To try and grasp the limits of "cyber" thought, to draw our revolutionaries out of the technological sleep into which they seem to have sunk, one must begin by framing differently the problem of the new supposedly "autonomous" machines. Above all, one must try and understand why the war machine takes precedence over the technical machine, why automation and decision making, the depersonalization of power relations by technology and political strategy are not mutually contradictory. On the contrary, technology favors decision making and strategy.

With each wave of innovation, we're told again that technology will "free up time," that the increasing productivity of the systems of machines will end up emancipating us from the necessity of labor. Now, not only are these promises of liberation never realized, but they are everywhere reversed into their opposite. Why? Quite simply because the machine must itself be delivered from its subordination. In capitalism, says Simondon, "The machine is a slave that serves to make other slaves."[22] This statement places us on the decisive path of power relations. For if the machine is a slave, it has an autonomy and independence that are completely relative; it must have a boss, a slave master, someone for whom it works and whose orders it executes. Simondon doesn't reveal to us the identity of that master, but Gilles Deleuze and Félix Guattari give us part of the answer: "We are always slaves of the social machine and never of the technical machine." The technical machine would therefore be subordinated to the war machine. It is the latter that gives form to the man-machine relation, for it precedes both the man and the machine, transforming the first into "variable capital" and the second into "fixed capital." We will follow this thread in order to reopen the debate around the relationship between war and revolution.

Marx and the Triple Power of the Machine, Science, and Nature

To try and grasp the nature and function of technology, one must also critique most of the Marxian observations concerning machines and their relationship with human beings. In *Capital*, Marx explains that the skilled work of the operator acting alongside machines is "devoid of any meaning" and represents an insignificant quantity opposite the powers of *science*, the *labor* incorporated into the system of machines, and the forces of *nature*. This "triple master," as Marx calls it, is based on a problematical conception of technology and its relation to man: the theory of commodity fetishism. It is of no help for understanding cybernetic machines. On the contrary. It remains completely anthropocentric, animated by "individuated" (living) subjects, reified (dead) objects, and (dialectical) mechanisms that overthrow relations between men, turning them into relations between things. It is this subject/object dialectic that gives rise to the idea of the automatic and impersonal operation of capitalist apparatuses that would alienate and dominate the men who have produced them; it is this idea that creates the illusion that strategic confrontations, war, power relations can be fully incorporated into the objectivity and impersonality of money, labor, law, consumption, social norms, algorithms, and finance.

A theory of machines based on an ontology of "individuated" subjects and "reified" objects, on the power of impersonal automatisms deriving from the dialectical reversal of the order of subjectivity into the order of objectivity will never be able to account for the nature of technology, which, as Simondon explains, "does not belong either to the pure social domain, nor to the pure physical domain:"[23] it emerges from the preindividual domain and the transindividual domain, evading individuated subjects as well as reified objects.

The evolution of the man-machine relationship, which Simondon constructs beyond the subject-object opposition, enables one to grasp the limits of contemporary theories: thanks to their cybernetic plasticity, machines would simulate the plasticity of the brain while acquiring an autonomy (Catherine Malabou) comparable to that of the human being; mathematical automatisms—algorithms—would constitute a new governmentality. The French philosopher's theory of machines allows us to criticize another, even stranger, theory, according to which the "cognitive" worker would have incorporated machines (fixed capital) into their subjectivity. Henceforth the "appropriation" of the means of production by workers, which in the past implied revolution, seizure of power, civil war, etc., would now be produced miraculously, without a hitch and without the capitalists even noticing it. The technical process by which the human body would produce artificial organs by externalizing those functions, would be inverted by the cognitive worker, who would have internalized the technology and the knowledge that produces it and makes it function. But it's a very different body that is summoned by technology: the "machine must be immediately conceived in relation to the social body and not in relation to a human biological organism."[24]

It is the "social body" of capitalism that distributes the technical machine as constant capital and the worker as variable capital. They are complementary, they evolve together, in parallel, under the control of the higher unity of the war machine. It's only from the standpoint of another "social body," that of revolution and its modes of organization, that capital's war machine can be critiqued and the relation between human and non-human can be configured differently.

Genealogy of the Machine

Simondon, like Deleuze and Guattari, defends another ontogenesis of technology. The machine does not extend the corporeal schema; "neither for the workers nor for the owners of the machines" is the machine an "organ," a prosthesis, an externalization of the arm, the eye, bodily strength, the brain, etc. It is not a tool. It is an assemblage, a coupling, an organization of two modes of existence (man and machine) which, we will add, develops under the constraint of the war machine that generated them. For Deleuze-Guattari and Simondon, the distinction between machine and tool is fundamental: instruments and tools being a prosthesis, a corporeal externalization, they don't have any "individuality" of their own, unlike the machine.

The 18th century is the century of the great development of tools and instruments. During that period, it was man that constituted the "technical individual" because he lent his "biological individuality" to technical individuation by wielding the tools and he constituted the center of that process. In contrast, the 19th century was the century of machines, which brought about a decentering of human functions. With capitalist industry, man was relieved of the function of "technical individual:" the tools were wielded by the machine (machine-tool), so that thenceforth it was the machine that occupied the center of technical individuation. The activity of the automatic machines was not *autonomous*, but *parallel* with human activity, which did not disappear, but shifted: its role was now to act beneath ("servant") or above ("regulator") the technical individual (machine). Man became either the organizer of relations between the technical levels—instead of being one of the levels himself—or simply a "supplier of elements" for the proper functioning of the machine.

These are the machines that one finds in *Capital*. The theories of the "triple master" and commodity fetishism are constructed on the basis of the automatic machines (machines-tools) of the 19th century, which have little in common with the contemporary cybernetic or self-regulating machines in which the function of the human changes once more. Whereas the Marxian automatic machines "need man as servant (worker) or organizer (capitalist), the self-regulating machines need man as technician, as associate,"[25] Simondon explains. The machines-tools become technical individuals only with these cybernetic machines.

The cybernetic machine, as a "technical individual," is not a thing, a mere object, nor an objectification of human activity, but a "mode of existence" that is added to and functions in parallel with the human mode of existence (neither of these parts can function autonomously, independently of the other). "Mode of existence" signifies that the machine is not an "absolute unity," a "closed block," a "substance"—that is, an already individuated, already complete, dead "thing," to use the language of Marx. The machine is open in several ways because it is relation and a multiplicity of relations: a relation to its own components, to other machines, to the world (the environment) and to the human. This being of technology, which Heidegger sought in vain, is therefore, for Simondon, relation. It "resides in the fact that the relation has the value of being: it has a doubly genetic function, vis-à-vis man and vis-à-vis the machine,"[26] while in contemporary critical thinking, "the machine and man are already entirely constituted and defined." Like Deleuze and Guattari, Simondon never treats man and machine as essences that would each lead an autonomous existence.

Man and machine are an assemblage [*agencement*], hence a field of possibilities, of virtualities as much as constituted elements (mechanical parts, software programs, algorithms), but all of that must be framed in relation to the possibilities and constituted elements of the war machine. If the machine is open, if the machine is relation, it contains a "margin of indetermination" and its individuation is not already given once and for all, for its functioning is adaptable and not rigidly constituted, like that of the automatons Marx speaks of, which are an inferior type of technology for that reason.

In substantializing the machine as a crystallization of "living labor," Marx conceives of it as a finished object, a "closed block," something "dead" ("dead labor" to be precise) having exhausted every potential, whereas all capacities are concentrated in living labor. In truth, however, the machine is defined not only by its current material state, but also by its invisible dimensions (plans, diagrams, etc.) and its potentialities. It is not dead, but very much "alive," subject to variation, change, capable of entering into different processes of individuation. If we understand the machine as relation, we can no longer utilize the Marxian categories of "living" (subjectivity) and "dead" (objectivity)—absolutely not, and the same goes, it should be said, for the Foucauldian category of the biological "living."

The War Machine

The set of relations that constitute the man-machine assemblage is caught in the individuation carried out by what Simondon calls, in a generic way, the "output civilization," which subjugates (enslaves) man and the machine to "productivity" and the domination of nature. It is here that the concept of war machine must be called into play. By reason of its indetermination, the machine (like the human, moreover) is open to an individuation that depends on the "social body" of capital.

Capitalism makes possible both the relative autonomy of technical machines and their brutal "slavery." Capital causes a rupture in political and social history, but also in the history of technics, by deterritorializing the monetary, social, technical, and political flows, which, in precapitalist societies were "embedded, coded, overcoded in such a way that they never become independent."[27] The generalized decoding of flows gave a new "freedom" and "independence" to the evolution of technical and scientific flows which at the same time were subjected to the logic of profit and power. So it is in capitalism, understood as a social machine performing this generalized decoding of flows, that the reasons for the development of techniques are to be sought: "It was not machines that created capitalism, in this sense, but capitalism, rather, that created machines, and that doesn't cease to introduce new breaks by which it revolutionizes its technical modes of production."[28]

Machines constitute themselves at the intersection of a dual, phylogenetic and ontogenetic, dimension. Technical machines enter into the "phylum" (the evolution) of the machines that preceded them and the virtualities of the machines to come. This phylum is not the bearer of a univocal historical causality since, thanks to the decoding of flows, the evolutive lines are rhizomatic, and several bifurcations are possible. But these relatively indeterminate possibilities of development are immediately captured and actualized by the war machine of capital. Going back to an example that we've already considered, the utilization of steam machines by the social machine of the Chinese Empire was very limited (children's toys), whereas the capitalist social machine made it the key element in its rise. It's not from a lack of conceptualization of capital that one can maintain that technical machines revolutionized the capitalist machine. Capital's diachronic machine, forced to undergo repeated ruptures ("crises") to be able to continually displace the limits of its valorization, "[never] lets itself be revolutionized by one or more synchronous technical machines."

The capitalist war machine "lets scientists and mathematicians 'schizophrenize' in their corner"— that is, it lets them follow and develop the phylum of their own discipline and in this way "channel socially decoded flows which they organize into axiomatics of purportedly basic research." However, the war machine inexorably subjects these flows of research and innovation to "a social axiomatic much more severe than all the scientific axiomatics, but also much more severe than all the old codes and overcodings that have disappeared: the axiomatic of the global capitalist market."[29]

Deleuze and Guattari precisely define the men/machines relationship within the operation of capital's war machine. The latter, in a state of permanent crisis (the machine "constantly goes haywire," always needs "social organs of decision making, management, reaction, inscription, a technocracy and a bureaucracy that are not reduced to the functioning of technical machines." The "management" of crises is not accomplished through the intervention of automatic apparatuses, but through the action of a technocracy and a bureaucracy that act as a subjectification of the megamachine of capital. As for these crises, which are never strictly economic, they always open up the possibility of civil war, so that the fascists may also intervene, in addition to the bureaucrats and technocrats.

The war machine never has an impersonal operation, even when it seems to function automatically, since "the bureaucrats and the technocrats" are always adjacent to the technical and social automatisms, ready to intervene when it breaks down, politically or economically. The politicians, technocrats, journalists, military men, experts, fascists, etc., constitute the subjectifications of the megamachine; they intervene as regulators, guardians, servants, restorers of the great flow of money, capital, technology, and war, but also as "governors" of the divisions of sex, race, and class, guarantors of the enslavements and subjugations implied by these divisions.

Subjectivities choose, make decisions, but these decisions and these choices are meant to establish or re-establish the functioning of the machine.

They apply strategies which the war machine implies, which it imposes when it malfunctions, but which only a subjectification can set right. During a collapse like that of 2008, the "automatisms" of the economy, the institutions, the laws, the technologies couldn't reproduce the power relations. And one could see, in practice, that the closing down of the multiplicity of relations constituting capital's machine is the outcome of strategy.

The Machine and the Ability to Revolt

Catherine Malabou gets things wrong twice: a first time in *Que faire de notre cerveau?* [*What Do We Do With Our Brain?*], because she assumes a difference in nature between humans (the plasticity of the human brain) and machines (computers), and a second time in *Métamorphoses de l'intelligence* [*Metamorohoses of the Intellect*], which was aimed at correcting the previous book by assuming a "structural sameness" of the brain and the computer. Simondon, like Guattari, formulates the problem very differently: in order to conceptualize the man-machine assemblage, one must go beyond the dualisms of nature and artifice, of the human and the non-human, but this doesn't mean that the components of the assemblage possess a "structural sameness."

"Subjectivity" is not an exclusive property of the human, but it is distributed in a different way in the human and in the machine. "There is something living in the technical ensemble,"[30] Simondon will say; Guattari, in turn, will speak, not of a "vital autonomy" of the machine ("it is not an animal"), but of a *"proto-subjectivity,"* a *"partial subjectivity"* endowed with a "singular power of enunciation"[31] that functions as a vector of subjectification.

The structural identity of man and the machine would imply that the components of the technical assemblage would have the same autonomy, the same capacity of acting. Simondon challenges this with a completely political argumentation because it centers on a specific form of acting: "refusal." "The technical being is more than a tool and less than a slave; it possesses an autonomy, but a relative, limited autonomy, without any real exteriority in relation to man who has constructed it."[32] The proto-subjectivity or partial subjectivity of machines is thus very different from human subjectivity, and Simondon defines it by the machine's inability to say no, to refuse. "The best calculating machine doesn't have the same degree of reality as an ignorant slave, because the slave can revolt whereas the machine cannot."[33]

Simondon doesn't ask himself whether the machine is capable of intervening when a "breakdown," an interruption, a malfunction occurs, nor whether it can repair itself (a conviction that Malabou, on the other hand, shares with the cyberneticians). The machine may be able to successfully perform all these activities, it can "go haywire and then present characteristics analogous to the crazy behavior of a living being," but it cannot bring about a "conversion" of its subjectivity, as the slave does when he rebels. By his refusal, the slave produces "a profound transformation of purposeful behaviors and not a behavioral malfunction." This refusal is not a simple breakdown, but a subjective rupture that problematizes existence and enables a change of its purposes.

"The machine is not self-creating." It can self-regulate, it can learn, but the adaptation remains insufficient to account for the self-creation which, proceeding via "abrupt leaps" and sudden ruptures, involves a conversion of subjectivity that creates "new possibles." Although the machine can solve problems, it is not capable of positing its "existence" and placing it under discussion.[34]

In this theory of machines, domination and refusal don't come under biopolitics. In Simondon and Guattari alike, the machine as relation implies a concept of the "living" that is not reducible to the biological, as is still the case in Agamben or Esposito. If the slave, like every living being, is a *biological automaton*, it is not on the basis of those organic automatisms necessary to life that he refuses and rebels, but on the basis of his non-organic potential [*puissance*]. "The automaton can be the functional equivalent of life, because life comprises functions of automatisms, self-regulation, and homeostasis, but the automaton can never be the equivalent of the individual."[35]

Refusal and revolt are not just interruptions. The cyberneticians and Malabou think that cybernetic machines can "interrupt their own automaticity" and simulate human subjectivity in that way. "Machines deliberately malfunction to better re-evaluate their operation" and "reorganization after the breakdown or interruption increases the efficiency of the automatism," allowing it to reach new thresholds of regulation."[36] The self-regulating "market," capable of repairing itself and repairing the damage of economic crises, is still the model of this thinking about technology.

But "the most ignorant" slave refuses and interrupts in a radically different way. He interrupts the automatisms that regulate his servitude so as to neutralize their power and assuredly not to improve their functioning, to achieve homeostasis, equilibrium. He interrupts in order to open up the possibility of converting his subjectivity and thus creating new orientations and new living conditions against his exploitation and his servitude. His revolt is anorganic and a-biological. It is here that govern-mentality comes into play, a governmentality whose basic function is to prevent, neutralize, undo "revolution," and which is therefore a politics of the anorganic. It is not just what intervenes in the life of the species, looking after illness and health, life and death, but, much more fundamentally, what decides concerning the possible and the impossible.

The main objective of a revolutionary war machine is to thwart this articulation by means of a rupture that suspends the laws of the capitalist machinery, in particular the distribution of the possible and the impossible that it implies, by creating new possibilities of action. To make possible what is impossible in the order of the capitalist machine ("Let's be realistic, let's demand the impossible!"), destruction and creation are complementary, which means that in order for the war machine to realize the "mutation," the conversion of subjectivity and the supersession of capitalism, it must also have as its aim "war" against capital. And this "war" must also liberate the machine, inseparable from the human.

One of the major reasons for the failure of the socialist revolutions of the 20th century lies in the understanding and utilization of machines and workers. Socialism (and Marxism), exactly like capital, substantializes and materializes the multiplicity of relations that constitute the technical machine, having it "coincide with its current state, with its material determinations." This is why, while making technology a focus of the revolution (the "Soviets plus electrification"), the Soviet Union never managed to imagine an alternative to capitalism. The "margin of indetermination" of the man-machine relationship was submitted to productivity, which enslaves man, the machine, and nature. The socialist state was content to copy the capitalist model by *accelerating* the application of Taylorism and by making the "Stakhanovist worker" an appendage of productivity. Thus, it reduced machines to the status of things and elevated the workers to the rank of "demiurges," while making nature an object of domination.

Automation and Decision Making

"According to Bergson, the growing complexity of the organism is essentially due to the necessity of complicating the nervous system, because the greater complexity of the cerebral and nervous system leads to a larger interval between action and reaction. And what does this complication consist of? It consists of a *simultaneous development of automatic activity and voluntary activity*. There is no opposition between the two orders of development, for the automatic provides the 'appropriate instrument' to the will."

— *Vidéophilosophie*

Simondon shows the inconsistency of the idea that the machine can acquire its own autonomy by simulating the living. From the point of view of machines, from the strictly technological point of view, pure automatisms don't exist: "The adequate relation to the technical object must be grasped as a coupling between living and non-living. The pure automatism, excluding man and mimicking the living, is a myth [...]. There is no machine of all the machines."[37] If the automatisms do exist, their nature can only be socio-political, says Simondon—that is, conceived and constructed by the war machine, we will say. The automatisms (norms, laws, market) always result from a strategy, a project, a will to domination, a will to power.

Grégoire Chamayou also refutes this point of view in his analysis of the automation of warfare: "The political error would be in fact to believe that automatization is automatic in itself."[38] If the technical machine can be automatic, the war machine has reduced it to this operation that *is never automatic*. The installation of networks, instead of "decentralizing" power, helps to concentrate it even more. Instead of making subjectivity disappear, if the "theoreticians of the 'networked war'" thought that these new technologies were going to enable a decentralization of command, "in actual fact, so far the experience of pilotless systems proves the opposite." Instead of "'man' in general losing control in favor of the 'machine,' here it is the subaltern operators who lose (even more) autonomy in favor of the higher echelons of the hierarchy. An integral robotization would further reinforce this tendency towards the centralization of decision making, although under different, more discreet modalities, more economical certainly, but no less hypertrophied."[39]

Translating the imperative "target only legitimate targets" or "define a threshold of proportionality between civilians killed and expected military benefits," into the drone's digital program implies that "the parameters of the decision [are] specified, and this specification is not made by the program itself. This requires a choice in advance, a decision about the parameters of the decision—a *decision about the decision*. The centralization of command—even of this would now occur more through programmatic specifications than through orders—would thus assume inordinate proportions." If the automatic machine (the drone) must perform a task according to the "Minimum Carnage" variable, "what is the value corresponding to the variable [...]? One doesn't know. More than twenty civilians killed? O.K. But this little decision about the decision, made in a word or a keystroke, has expansive, concrete—all-too concrete—effects."[40]

These new technologies eliminate or displace the "very imperfect" links that connected the technical machine to the war machine, but this doesn't in any way signify a "horizontalization" of power relations. As we will see, contrary to what Boltanski at Chiapello or Dardot and Laval think, the same thing happens in the corporation and in finance. If the automatic apparatuses give workers, in the corporation, the "possibility of escaping the tyranny of the little bosses" by eliminating a few intermediate hierarchical echelons, they subject them to a much more tyrannical and formidable power.

The "automatic piloting" which the technological systems put in place to accelerate market operations don't make the hierarchies and their command disappear, but strengthen their decision-making capacity. There are no machines of machines (contrary to what Anders thinks) and there are no automatic pilots that govern society or the stock market. The automatic machine centralizes decision making even further: instead of abolishing it, it exalts it. It gives still more power to the higher levels of the hierarchy. Machines, including automatic ones, always depend on an exterior element. Machines and humans are part of collective assemblages (social machine and war machine) that produce and reproduce them together. "The problem is not to know who, man or machine, has the control. That is an underdetermined formulation of the problem. What is really in question is the material and political automatization of that 'band of armed men' that is first of all the state machinery."[41] We will say rather that it is a matter of the war machine of capital, of which the state is just one articulation, and that automatization is the technological realization of capital's strategy of "secession." A strategy that, as always, requires its subjectifications, its "armed bands."

The accelerationist, post-workerist, cyber-feminist theories are incapable of accounting for the relationship between decision making and automation, because they carefully avoid problema-tizing the capitalist war machine's strategies of confrontation (civil war) on which depends the actualization of the "possibilities" of technics and science. The juridical, economic, and technological automatisms will never be able to explain how and why the transition from Fordism to neoliberalism, the hegemony of financial capital over industrial capital, the management of the "financial crisis, the new mutations of fascism" came about. In order to grasp these turning points of history, these "subjective breaks," one must center the analysis not on the "possibilities" of the technologies and science, but on the strategic ruptures that orient the politics of science and technology.

One can even consider that these subjectifica-tions are slaves of the social "machine" and its laws, that they only serve the financial machine, that the different states are enslaved to capital's war machine.

The fact remains that, even in that case, the "guardians" of the social machine are adversaries, that they are waging a war and a civil war against the adversaries of the operation of the megamachine.

Simondon and Guattari have developed a very innovative theory of machines radically opposed to the Heideggerian conception of technology. But, like all the theoreticians of the 1960s and 1970s, after introducing domination, enslavement, and the strategic point of view, they sought highly improbable solutions to the war that is underway: Simondon emphasizes the creative side of the relation, as if the alienation—which he does thematize—were surmountable by invention alone; Guattari, who invented the concept of war machine, abandons it in his last works. The aesthetic paradigm that closes his research sanctions a separation between the war machine as mutation, creation, subjectification, and the war machine that aims to overcome capitalism. It's this second one that we need to reconnect with.

War Machine and Technical Machine in the Organization of Labor

The large corporate enterprise used to be the place where one could grasp the operation of capital and its political strategy, and, at the same time, the space where the revolutionary struggle was to be organized and deployed. Today one has the impression that there only remains a single strategy, that of the bosses, whom computer automation allows to centralize and reinforce the project of political separation which the cybernetic machines carry to their last consequences. The organization of labor seems to have crossed a new threshold of abstraction that profoundly affects the subjectivity of workers.

Marie-Anne Dujarier[42] describes prescription and command in the organization of labor of the large enterprise as a "management through apparatuses," which can also be defined as a "management without managers," since these latter operate "at a distance" from production to orient the behaviors of the wage-earners, without knowing anything about the work and the workers, according to the principles of "abstract labor." Dujarier applies to workers and consumers the idea of governmentality at a distance developed by Foucault in regard to the population. The population is actualized essentially through informational apparatuses that dictate what should be done, at what rhythm, following what procedure, and with what quality. All these apparatuses are conceived and fabricated by what the author calls "*planneurs/planeurs*"—first, because they think and organize the work in terms of "plans," considering the activity as being decomposable and recomposable according to a linear and rational model, and, second, because they "plane" or hover over the concrete work.

What interests us is the concept of apparatus [*dispositif*] which Dujarier takes up again from Foucault (and Agamben) and which we will redeploy in light of the division between technical machine and war machine. While considering apparatuses as things, as objects that mediate relations between men, she defines them as "machines." The "apparatus" (the machine) is a slave that serves to create other slaves (workers). One can add, in this context, that the apparatus is constructed by still other slaves, "degree-holding and well-paid" but whose intelligence, knowledge, and skills are managed, exploited, and subordinated by the abstract labor machine for the purposes of performance, productivity, and rationality commanded and prescribed by the management. In the organization of contemporary labor, the "enterprise" (which can just as well be an automobile factory as a school, an institution monitoring the unemployed as a hospital, a supermarket as a law court) seems to have found a strategy, apparatuses, and power relations for *establishing its separation from the workers*.

In a very striking way, Dujarier calls the contemporary modes of organization of labor "relationless social relationships," by which she means tasks, functions, and behaviors that are imposed unilaterally by the directors through apparatuses conceived by the *planneurs*, the program managers. These "relationless social relationships" register both the workers' extreme weakness, their inability to establish and impose a relation of force with the employers and the power of the capitalist initiative which only meets with weak resistances, routinely and easily swept aside.

The program managers are thus the keystone of the strategy of secession. They have the task of organizing the teamwork, of standardizing, prescribing, assessing, controlling the labor power through computer apparatuses[43] in order to improve the performance as defined by the directors, while establishing a physical, temporal, organizational, and affective distance from production. This strategy of "separation" was made possible by the nature of contemporary capital which, unlike the capitalism of Marx, is not oriented toward production,[44] but, immediately, toward "shareholder value." The criteria and the measure of the productivity of enterprises are no longer defined by industry, but by finance.

Unlike Taylor, who was originally a worker, and managers of the Taylorist era, who had an intimate knowledge of industrial work, the apparatuses of remote governmentality are fabricated without any knowledge of the work and the workers. What the programmers, veritable workers in abstraction, manipulate, through their "plans," methods, software, are numbers, prices, headcounts, costs, statistics. The manipulation of abstractions is all the easier as they don't make "reference to any concrete situation."

Compared to Taylorist management, the program managers perform an abstraction squared, so to speak, disconnected from the work and the workers, in order to construct this power machine. One of them declares for example: "I've never heard any talk about work here. One talks about management, process, end-to-end, performance, but never about work. Me, I've never organized people's work. I've dealt with procedures, mesurements, disparities, and that's all. I've never meddled with their work. I worry because in fact I don't know their job and don't have any expertise. I know the machinery, but not the work. I don't have access to what they do. I have no sense of it." The program managers "don't have any occupation" and yet they "prescribe the occupation of others," affirms a woman interviewee. In reality they do have an occupation, an *occupation of all occupations*, one could say, capable of extracting abstract labor from no matter what activity and of "optimizing" the "abstract values" that result from it.

Carrying out this fundamental task implies an "indifference" to every content, which is manifested in a radical way in the contemporary enterprise. "I worked on a piece of production software, for the ham of brand X, but me, I don't know anything about ham. I had to work on the program that allows the guys to track the production line, the management of stock, etc. But personally I have never seen a ham production line in my life."

The "distance" that is taken from the work in no way means that the production process is now in the hands of workers, that the teamwork, instead of being imposed by the capitalist, expresses the autonomy of workers having incorporated the machines, as is believed in an utterly incomprehensible way by my comrades of cognitive capitalism. In capitalism, autonomy and independence must be wrested away from and imposed on the war machine of capital. They have no "ontological" substance. Like the "unlettered" workers of the 19th century, contemporary workers—cognitive or not—have to assert their independence and their autonomy *politically*; without a refusal of work, they are nothing but an element of capital ("human capital," the modernized version of "variable capital"), nothing but parts of the productive machine, at the service of the "boss."

While the word "work" is practically absent from the language of the program managers, "on the other hand, the measuring of labor power is omnipresent, whether it's a matter of its cost, its quality, or its value." Prescription and standardization are accompanied by a constant and obsessive evaluation, put in place by the upper management

and having to be supplied by the workers themselves. Evaluation and the apparatuses are aimed at
measuring the unmeasurable, transforming quality
into quantity, getting quantity to emerge from
quality. What is impossible to measure is "living
labor," not at all abstract labor. The program
managers are well aware that "real labor" is irreducible to "prescribed labor," that in the action's
unfolding, "the hazy, the unpredictable, the illogi-
cal, the non-rational" are indispensable to the
accomplishment of any labor. They know perfectly
well that abstraction doesn't make the concrete or
living labor disappear, since the "abstract labor" is
extracted from it. However, setting "real labor"
against "prescribed labor," "living labor" against
"abstract labor," without a "refusal of work," without affirming a hostility to capital, is a political
strategy that has no chance of succeeding, since the
dialectic of the two terms is already incorporated
into the organization of labor.

The Vampire of Subjectivity

The functioning of the war machine (like that of
the technical machine) isn't possible without the
intervention of different subjectivities. Capital
needs to suck up subjectivity like the vampire
sucks blood. The contemporary capitalist enterprise

shows clearly that the automatism of the apparatuses is not itself automatic, but that it needs to be conceived, fabricated, maintained, and accepted by a multiplicity of subjectivities, "enslaved" to varying degrees, but which all participate in this process that subjugates the technical machine and the human to the machinery of the enterprise.

First, the "automatic apparatus" has to be included in the strategic plans of the enterprise and be prescribed by its management to the program managers (decision, subjective act). Next, it must be produced by the latter, who translate the desires of the board of directors and senior managers into technologies, signs, procedures, and protocols. The remote managers are succeeded by the operational managers, who are responsible for getting the apparatus to function in production in such a manner that it is maintained by the workers, improved, and adapted to the contingency of the situation (direct command over persons). Abstract labor is not imposed on concrete labor as a fate, it is never the reversal of human activity into the impersonal action of things; it results from a strategy deliberated by the management which mobilizes different subjectivities and combines machines and men, humans and non-humans (machines, signs, procedures), every step of the way.

Management itself is organized according to a strict division of labor that subjects the program managers' subjectivity to a reduction, a mutilation, and an exploitation equivalent in many respects to those imposed on wage-workers assigned to production. Program managers are part of the management personnel. Yet they "describe themselves as 'cogs' in the great productive machine" and "speak of themselves as dominated, reified, manipulated, salaried workers," they see themselves as "dominated dominants," which may be the most revealing and exact definition. They nonetheless constitute an articulation of a new type of "boss" composed of different functions. Marie-Anne Dujarier names seven of these types: "private or public owners, members of the board of directors, salaried directors, specialized program managers, local supervisors, financial intermediaries, and finally, providers of managerial products." Different logics preside over the functions and subjectivities of management, but the "articulations" between them and the "arbitrages," the decisions, the strategic choices, are, as in the enterprises of former times, in the hands of the "general management." Centralization of power remains the law of capitalist production, which goes, without any contradiction, by way of "decentralization."

The fabrication of management programs [*logiciels*] is subjected in turn to a very hierarchized division of labor (in "management in pieces," everyone does a specialized task which they can complete without mastering the project as a whole), organized according to a strategy which the programmers aren't familiar with and only partially understand ("I'm a pawn, an underling!," "They give me a guideline and I follow it.") These workers in abstraction, creators of "platforms" that can take a thousand forms (electronic information points, websites, information systems, etc.), work triply blind: as to the strategies of the company, the labor that they organize, and the construction of the apparatuses themselves, which they know and control only in part. The intelligence, the knowledge, and the know-how are subjected to the action of the war machine of abstract labor which dictates which knowledge, which skills, must be mobilized, in what framework, for what ends. The program managers don't have the "time to read, think, put things in perspective" outside their work. In order to "meet their obligations" they must avoid "thinking about certain aspects of their function," in the same way as a worker who works on the assembly line stops asking himself or herself questions about their situation so they can keep on doing it." Intelligence, creativity, and invention are practiced only within the limits established by the war machine of the enterprise. The "knowledges" are selected and formatted by the constraints of valorization. "Hence they are asked, required, to think within a frame," that of the rationalization and quantification of abstract labor. "But they can't consider the framing itself," the aims and modalities of abstract labor, "without running the risk of ineffectiveness and professional exclusion." The machine of the enterprise produces a dissociation and a training of the program managers' intelligence "an awkward, restrained intelligence outside the frame, and within the frame a second intelligence that is sharp, quick, combinatorial, and capable of creativity, of abstract virtuosity, [but] socially divided, prescribed, hierarchized, and controlled."

The intelligence of the program managers is essentially that of capital's war machine, of which they are the agents and the victims. Knowledge doesn't confer any autonomy and independence if it doesn't refuse the "framework" in which it functions, if it doesn't interrupt itself, if it doesn't halt the production of which it only constitutes a cog. It is only under these conditions that the General Intellect could be rescued from the logic of capitalist valorization, contrary to what the the theories of "cognitive [neuronal, computational, etc.] capitalism" claim, which conflate "knowledge" and "power," in the same way as the Social Democracy of the first half of the 20th century. Social Democrats "did not perceive the ambiguity in the slogan "Knowledge is power" [...] they believed that the same knowledge which secured the domination of the proletariat by the bourgeoisie would enable the proletariat to free itself from this domination. In reality, a form of knowledge which had no access to practice, and which could teach the proletariat nothing about its situation as a class, posed no danger to its oppressors."[45] The proletariat needs an altogether different kind of knowledge, a knowledge of struggles, in order to assert its political autonomy.

The setting-up of digital systems [*dispositifs*], their maintenance, their adaptation, and their improvement require the mobilization of other subjectivities: the intervention of different management functions (changeover specialists, cost controllers, computer engineers, consultants, auditors, trainers, service providers, private certifiers) and that of the workers themselves, so that what is deployed is never automatism itself, but the man-machine assemblage.

Further, maintenance of the apparatuses assumes a growing importance and involves subtracting more and more time from production ("the time devoted to maintaining the apparatuses themselves, hence deducted from productive labor time, can be estimated at at least 5% for the operationals, at least 50% for the local supervisors, and nearly 90% in the social headquarters"). The intensification of abstract labor takes the form of an apparatus that obliges the worker to furnish, in addition to more "productive" labor, an increasing labor of "anti-production," to speak like Deleuze and Guattari, labor that, from the capitalist viewpoint, even with the new modalities, continues to be offensive to the workers, since in terms of activity, the framing by apparatuses seems to produce numerous processes of underperformance." "They have trouble understanding why their employer spends so much money and ingenuity to discourage them from working."

In reality, from the capitalist point of view, this money is very well spent, for—this is the most innovative thesis of Marie-Anne Dujarier—there occurs a shifting of the center of activity away from the workers. The apparatuses, "in addition to being a patial automation of production, […] also automate the work of organization." However, unlike what happened with Taylorism, the abstraction musn't eliminate all activity (living or real labor) by reducing it to the status of mere execution, it must move the activity so that it is "centered on the managerial machine itself"—that is, in the last analysis, on the war machine. The program managers "don't want the workers to stop feeling, thinking, and signifying"; on the contrary, they call upon "the autonomy, the personality, the creativity of each one, so that these faculties may be used, 'beyond' the machine to correct it, repair it, adapt it in response to local situations." "The appeal to autonomy in a context where it appears to have disappeared would indeed signal a shift: the activity would be less oriented toward production than toward the apparatus itself," the enhancement of the managerial machine that produces "abstract labor."

Checking boxes, filling out evaluation grids, detailing what one has done in the most precise way, participating in meetngs to learn how to make the power machine run as the power machine: all these activities are equally applicable to the industrial worker, the university professor, the personnel of a hospital, or an institution of assistance to the poor. Making the apparatus itself function also constitutes the bulk of the labor imposed on the precarious workers of the "platforms." For a company like Uber, the service of transporting persons has less importance than the harvesting of information and the evaluations that drivers and customers are supposed to supply, albeit grudgingly.

Each level of the hierarchy requires a specific subjugation for sustaining the men-machines relation, but all of them need to answer to the machine of abstract labor. To define these activities of control, of domination, as parasitic, as useless, would be to miss the reality of capitalism, which is not just "production," but also power. And from time immemorial, the production and reproduction of power relations requires techniques, a certain amount of time, investments, and a certain number of "flunkies."

Dujarier's analysis of the large enterprise covers many but not all of the transformations that have completely reconfigured it. I would like to mention two others, basing myself on the Italian experience, where capital's initiative is even more advanced and the weakness of the workers is even more pronounced than in France.

In a historic project of naval construction where the power of communist workers was quite real (at the time of the founding of Yugoslavia by Tito, 3,000 shipyard workers who were living at its border, crossed that border to build "socialism" in the Yugoslav naval yards). The workforce went from 12,000 workers down to 1,200. Among those 1,200 employees, the workers were in the minority, since their work had been outsourced to subcontractors, who then outsourced it to other subcontractors. The workers of these different levels of subcontractors were of a dozen different nationalities (for example, 2,000 were from Bangladesh). Rights and security diminished as one descended in the hierarchy of subcontractors. The divisions of income, status, and race wiped out any "workers' power."

The heads of the large Italian companies are putting in place something that the French employers' confederation (the Medef) has always dreamed of;[46] company welfare is gradually replacing "universal' welfare, multiplying and further reinforcing the divisions within the workforce. The condition of the workforce of the large companies seem in this way to be returning to the beginnings of industrialization, when the paternalistic boss saw to the life of the workers from birth to death (another transformation of European biopolitics that escaped Foucault). Metalworkers, the spearhead of the workers' movement of the postwar years, have gone even further by accepting a branch agreement which, foreseeing a "corporative" welfare for workers of that sector, signs the death warrant of the "European model" and affirms the ascendancy of the American model.

The Corporate Enterprise as Origin and Source of Nihilism

Marie-Anne Dujarier's study lays out, without drawing all the consequences from it, the mortal dangers to which capital's war machine exposes the subjectivities that she models and the perils to which it exposes society and the world. The ability to treat any activity as abstract labor—that is, to extract quantifiable value from all activity, determines a radical "indifference" to every content, to every use value. The consequences of this "abstraction" are formidable, since the accumulation of capital is indifferent to everything, except to the quantitative limits that it must constantly surpass.

These dangers are not perceived by the program managers. On the contrary, abstraction would seem to have a "ludic" effect on them: having lost every connection to the singularity of situations and subjectivities, they see their ability to decompose and recompose gestures, tasks, and behaviors as a "game." In this regard, Dujarier speaks of the enthusiasm of a human resources manager on the announcement of a new mission, which will consist of "dismissing five hundred persons in three months without making a wave." For him, it's a "nice challenge." He says he's "excited" and "eager" to begin the job" which presents itself as a delicate equation, on which he will be able to deploy his intelligence and his acumen: "It's not a sure thing; it's interesting as a challenge." Now, this "entertaining," "fun," "amusing," or "interesting" relation of the program managers to their activity conceals a more violent and more dangerous relationship with the world and with others.

The process of selection/fabrication of a hyped intelligence in a framework that excludes an uncomfortable, thwarted, repressed intelligence denied the possibility of talking about this same framework, has already proved its worth during the two world wars, where the organization of labor reached an intensity and a scale that was unknown until then. The industrial extermination of the Jews during the Second World War was just the most ignoble result of capitalist streamlining, whose conditions of possibility are being reproduced, with no major differences, in the contemporary organization of labor. "Not seeing" was not an exceptional attitude, characteristic of the Nazis and no one else. The refusal to see the consequences of what one is engaged in is deeply ingrained in the scientific organization of work. It is constitutive of its functioning and its laws. The statements of the abstraction workers are damning in this regard.

In order to build a career, there is "a rule of the game that must be observed: insofar as possible, don't evoke the concrete dimension of the symbols that are manipulated on a daily basis." The program managers "don't need to know what is behind the numbers," because if they start to ask themselves questions and voice them out loud, the work slows down and they place their career in danger. "I don't have any idea of the impact I have on the reality of the work of people who will use this software package. And the question shouldn't be posed [...]. When one sells a management change, one applies a generic something or other to an organization, without wondering if it is meaningful or not. It's necessary not to ask oneself such things if you want to continue." To maintain the abstraction, it is essential to stay indifferent to everything that isn't streamlining, productivity, performance. In order to escape reality and contribute to the "social construction of indifference," the *planneurs* invent techniques: "I speed myself up to a certain level, where I'm no longer there, I've escaped reality, I'm no longer thinking. When I'm speeding along, I don't retain anything. Speeding is a way of avoiding feeling."

The capitalist organization of labor produces potential criminals who, like the Nazis during the Nuremberg trials, won't feel responsible for the outcome nor for their involvement in the "production," because for them, as for capital, all productions are the same, so long as they are efficient, rationally organized, and they meet the criteria of quantification and calculability. Like the Nazis, everyone will be able to repeat: "We have done our job," "We have followed orders." They act in and for the war machine of which they are both the actors and the victims. This is not a sleep of reason that produces monsters, but the "peaceful" organization of labor crossing another threshold in the social construction of nihilism.

The thesis of Günther Anders still seems pertinent, therefore. It can easily be applied to the recent generations of intellectual (or cognitive) workers. The changes in the organization of labor haven't weakened the responsibility of the capitalist enterprise in the production of "irresponsible" behaviors and subjectivity. The program managers are exposed to the same dangers as the authors of Nazi crimes, "who basically adopted the behavior to which they had been conditioned, habituated, by the corporate enterprise."[47]

For every entrepreneur, it's a matter of absolute "indifference" whether the product is cars, yogurts, sports events, furniture, or the health of the population. This indifference as to the content and the purposes of the product carries over into the work itself, which must also make an abstraction of all use value. The capitalist enterprise demands a "total commitment" of the worker, who must never concern himself with the purpose of the production. It establishes a strict separation between the *production* and the *product*: "The moral status of the product (the status of poison gas or that of the hydrogen bomb) doesn't cast any shadow over the morality of the worker who takes part in its production. "The most repugnant product cannot contaminate the work itself."[48] Labor, like the money of which it is the precondition, "has no odor." "No work can be discredited by its purpose."

The working man has taken the "secret oath" to "not see or rather not know what he was doing," to "not consider its purpose," to "not seek to know what he does." As the example of the *planneurs* has shown us, the "knowledge" of consequences isn't necessary for working. On the contrary: "His ignorance is preferred in the interest of the company. It would be false, however, to suppose that he would need to know. In fact, at least in the very act of working, a vision of the purpose (or even of the use to be made of this purpose, which in any case is already decided), would do him no good. It would even disturb him."[49]

The contemporary corporate enterprise tries to alleviate the nihilism it inevitably secretes by inventing an "ethics" for itself, but the "moral and moralizing" in which the managerial discourse is enveloped ("durable development," "diversity," "parity," "handicap," "citizenship," etc.) doesn't correspond to anything, because its only real law is that of profit, which is to say, ethical indifference.

Men are trained in "collaboration," not by an ideology, but by assemblages, apparatuses, practices, enslavements that aren't limited to that of labor. Today the consumer is not in the same position of "collaboration." He or she doesn't have to question themselves either about the modes of manufacture of the product (use of pesticides? exploitation of workers, children, and slaves?), or about the impacts which the manufacture and the consumption have on the planet. Consumption "has no odor" either—like labor, it really only serves to produce money. Hence, compared to

Anders' era, the problem has gotten even worse, for if the worker is indifferent to the *product*, the consumer is indifferent to the *production*. What must be questioned is not only the purposes of the product, but also the conditions of production and those of consumption, which contain both the reasons for the exploitation and the reasons for the ecological catastrophe. If it isn't to fail, the ecological struggle must presuppose the neutralization of the indifference that inheres in capitalist production and consumption. Indifference is not a psychological trait, but an objective and subjective condition of the production of capital.

Financial capital, the true "general management" of the enterprise, completes the process of abstraction and creation of indifference, since the financiers only know and manipulate the money abstraction with no concern for the use value of production. The "abstractions" of stock-market value secrete modes of subjectification whose acceleration can lead, like the abstractions of industrial value have already done, to new fascist subjectifications.

The rise of new fascisms creates the conditions for a truly "criminal" evolution of this indifference, as we observe when the death of thousand of migrants in the Mediterranean greet with the apathy of the European populations. The astonishing speed with which democracy can transform itself into fascism has its roots in the blindness produced by the division of labor and by consumption, which, to varying degrees, affects everyone. "Not seeing" and "not feeling" have spread in Europe without encountering any real obstacles.

Depersonalization or Class War?

It's claimed that the impact of "machines" in the organization of labor resides in an automatization that *depersonalizes* power relations by incorporating them in digital technologies and alogorithms that make them function. But depersonalization is completely relative, since it is constantly what is at issue in a class struggle, whose goal is precisely to expose the strategy beneath the autonomisms of the apparatuses, and the will to domination of certain "persons" (the bosses) over others (the workers) beneath the technology.

In the large industrial concentrations, the reality of power relations has not always been so "pacified" as it has been since the 1980s. Relations have not always had the form of governmentality. In the 1960s and at the beginning of the 1970s, a "shop-floor guerrilla warfare" animated power relations, so that the management and the technology manifested themselves as domination and repression. The emergence and consolidation of the workers' "war machines" had the ability to "unmask" the subjectivity of the command that was hiding behind the automatism of the assembly line, to name the will to domination that was lodged in the impersonality of the technology. The conflict inside the factory had turned into a strategic confrontation between adversaries and could end only with the victory of one side (the capitalists) and the defeat of the other (the workers)

The storytelling (Foucault, Chiapello-Boltanski, Dardot-Laval, etc.) about the advent of "humanistic" management in the factory and "pacified" governance in society is false, therefore. The idea that the "new spirit of capitalism" is able to integrate the criticism of its organization by incorporating the autonomy, independence, and self-affirmation demanded by the struggles of the 1960s into a new organization of labor only expresses the political wishes of its authors. In reality, it results from an enormous error of perspective since it applies to neoliberalism the logic of the the "reformist" dialectic of the postwar boom, the "*Trente Glorieuses*" (of which its authors are the nostalgic orphans), whereas neoliberalism's project is altogether different: a radical negation of any reformism, an imposition of "relationless social relationships," an unambiguous pursuit of the political secession of capital and its property.

Taking the global economy into consideration— that is, *the only dimension on the basis of which one can evaluate a power phenomenon*—we can say with certainty that these modes of humanistic management have involved only a tiny minority of enterprises: the "creative work" of the Silicon Valley (if there). And it's not an innovation, since, as we've seen, already at the beginning of the Cold War, the production of science and technology, under the leadership of the U.S. Army, was carried out through interdisciplinary teamwork in an atmosphere of conviviality. The new spirit of capitalism has never been realized in the large enterprises, where, on the contrary, there has been a proliferation, as in China, Korea, Japan, of suicides, humiliations, coercions, depressions, and even *"karoshi"* (death by overwork). The "actual results" of governmentality in the enterprise and in society are deplorable and ought to instruct us about what it is really governing: the trumph of capital and its project of secession. It is going down a path that its critics have trouble considering, by returning, as in Brazil, to its inaugural moments.

The changes in the organization of labor and society refer one back to the ruptures, the discontinuities, the strategies, that alone "make historical events decipherable." The "triumph in the combat against the subaltern classes" is what constitutes the key to the historical events of the end of the 20th century. Contrary to the analyses that explain changes by the creativity, autonomy, and independence of labor (or its recuperation by capital), Benjamin's warning against Social Democracy remains extremely relevant today. "Foreseeing the worst," along with Marx and Benjamin, one must object "*that man only possesses his labor capacity, that he can only be the slave of other men* [...] *who have made themselves owners.*"

Pursuing Benjamin's intuitions, Hans-Jürgen Krahl—also known for theorizing the mutation of intellectual labor—suggests that one mustn't just consider the working class as the "producer of capital," but also as a force that destroys capital. This second function is overlooked by the contemporary Marxist theories (including the theory of cognitive capitalism) that measures labor's revolutionary action in terms of its "productivity," its creativity, its "autonomy." The idea of "destructive force" dislodges the "economism" that often affects Marxism on the strategic terrain, by radicalizing, at the end of the 1960s, the concept of "labor as non-capital" (*Die Arbeit als das nict-Kapital*) and the concept of "political refusal of capital" of Mario Tronti. Revolutionary action is *destruction* of the capitalist power relationship that engenders the boss and the workers at the same time. But post-workerism makes the opposite wager: it abandons the strategic perspective of the revolutionary years, by exalting the "productive force" and expelling all negativity from the action of labor power.

According to it, the historical defeat of the working class actually produced a victory of labor power, because the capitalist enterprises "are no longer capable of centralizing the productive forces and of integrating labor power as they did in the age of big industry."[50]

This description of the relations of force between classes is counterintuitive; the reality seems to function in exactly the opposite way, particularly in the enterprises and on the labor market, as we've shown above. But, say these theoreticians, in contemporary biopolitics, labor power, unlike industrial production, "shows its autonomy, its increasing ability to organize networks and organizational forms [...] its growing capacity to self-manage production," while capital has been reduced to simple command, which "weakens productivity," blocks the production power of the cognitive workers.

Separation, autonomy, and independence being already realized by labor power, the latter doesn't even need to exert its "destructive force" nor to subjectify itself into a political class. It is autonomous and separate "in itself." Capital, "incapable of integrating labor power,"[51] is divided into two antagonistic subjectivities that are opposed in a radical way, prior to any conflict, to any political rupture. Without our realizing it, we are in a situation of dual power. In industrial production, revolutionary rupture is necessary for "the one to divide in two"; in biopolitical power, the "one divides in two" in advance of any "destructive" action.

The abandonment of the strategic viewpoint of the first workerism [*operaismo*] and the insistence on a completely positive labor power requires a different foundation than a discontinuance of confrontation given the relation of capitalist domination. Underpinning class war, underpinning the always singular struggle, there is a philosophy of history which, having gone out through the front door, has come back through the little window of the "progress" of labor power. Historicism, denied in principle, is actually completely assumed when one asserts that the cognitive worker possesses, unlike the worker of the plantations and that of big industry, a "cognitive autonomy" which the capitalist has been obliged to accept and with which he is obliged to negotiate. In reality, the history of labor power doesn't appear to have the goal and the direction that is attributed to it, nor to proceed linearly toward its fulfillment, the cognitive worker. Both the slave and the worker of big industry have expressed a political power by attacking the relation of subordination thanks to their "destructive force," which the "cognitive workers" are incapable of mobilizing precisely because they have lost all negativity, precisely because they are "production" first of all, "cooperation" first of all, "force of invention" first of all.[52] "Negotiation" (or more likely, the refusal to negotiate—since neoliberalism is precisely an anti-reformism, there is nothing to negotiate!) doesn't at all occur on the basis of cognitive autonomy, but on that of political rupture, uprising, the application of destructive force, as all the political movements since 2011, including the recent Yellow Vests, have shown.

The destructive force mustn't just be aimed at the "masters," but also at the "slaves" and their activities, from which the form of "productivity," of "labor," of "consumption" must be removed, as they are still too close to the power one wishes to rid oneself of. The destructive force also has to be summoned because in reality we don't have a "double production of subjectivity" that neatly separates labor power and capital. Without the revolutionary rupture, the workers (like everyone, moreover) are caught in power relations that, instead of having the form of antagonism, have that of complicity, collaboration, participation in the great disaster of capitalist production. The destructive force doesn't just have the function of neutralizing capital's domination, but of creating the conditions of a conversion of subjectivities, of the necessary change of their modes of cooperation and action, since even the forms of resistance bear the stamp of the enemy.

The category of destructive labor seems therefore much more promising than the concept of productive labor to which Marxism has devoted rivers of ink. Especially seeing that Krahl doesn't limit this power of destruction to workers, but broadens it to include all those who contribute to that "ethical" activity. It is only on the basis of this "destructive character" that one can again think of rupture and revolution.

3

Becoming-Revolutionary and Revolution

But the problem is revolution![1] The word "revolution" has disappeared from political programs and theoretical reflections, while throughout the 20th century up to the 1960s, it enabled the workers' movement to keep the initiative and maintain a strategic advance over capital.

The 20th century was the century of wars, civil wars, and revolutions. From 1905 in Russia to the revolution in Iran (1979) and in Central America (1990), going by way of Mexico (1910), Europe following the Great War (Germany, Italy, Hungary, etc.), China (1949), Asia (1954, etc.) Africa (1962, etc.), the Caribbean and South America (Cuba, etc.), 1968 (Mexico, France, Czechoslovakia, etc.), the planet experienced a series of uprisings and revolutions unprecedented in the history of humanity.

In the 19th century, all the revolutionary attempts took place in the West and all of them failed. What's worse, they ended in massacres, like that of the Paris Commune, which fired the imagination of the proletarians and cadres of the workers' movement. For the bourgeoisie there could be no question of the "capital of the 19th century" becoming the theater of a revolutionary experience.

Lenin's rupture with this tradition involved the construction of a party (on the hierarchical model of the factory, according to Max Weber), of a type of militant subjectivity (the "professional revolutionary"), and a method (the class consciousness carried to the exterior by a vanguard), whose purpose was the seizure of power. Since the revolutionary desires and projects had shattered against two main reefs—power and war, Lenin supplied a solution that proved very effective: take power by transforming imperialist war into class war on the basis of a subject conceived as autonomous, the working class placing itself athwart the course of history (or of historicism).

But two decisive changes made impracticable the Leninist and Maoist answers to the question "What is to be done?" First, the new modalities of total war and civil wars, continuing in the New Deal and the Cold War, sketched out a new capitalism that the Marxists continued to interpret with the categories of the 19th century; second, the emergence, in the postwar period, of new political subjects—the colonized, women, students—bearers of new modes of exploitation, domination, and political action.

The "strange revolution" of the 1960s was a decisive moment: unable to find a solution to the problem it had raised (socialism is only a form of capitalism), it ended with a historic failure. We are still not done with this failure because the old forms of organization and struggle that ensured independence and political autonomy are no longer practicable, while the questions to which they were able to give a response are still and always present, but they only give rise to local inventions and experimentations of short duration that don't trouble capitalism.

In a quite arbitrary way, I will set out the conditions that led to the "disappearance" of the revolution through a convocation of four authors, Frantz Fanon, Mario Tronti, Carla Lonzi, and Hans-Jürgen Krahl, whom I will consider (arbitrarily again) as expressing the perspectives of the movements of the colonized, of "workers," of women, and of students, respectively. The viewpoints of these "militants" have a different consistency than those of the professional philosophers, to which it is interesting to compare them.

In the 19th Century, Revolution Is Global for the First Time

Revolution was born bourgeoise in France; it became proletarian and haunted Europe, but it was only by moving, first toward the east and then toward the south, that it would become global. This cycle of revolutions begun by the Bolsheviks has provoked heated discussions. Gramsci's statement that "the events of 1917 are the last occurrence of this kind in the history of politics," is obviously false because valid only for the North. It was proved wrong throughout the 20th century by the series of revolutions on a world scale that was unique in number and intensity. But the possibility of world revolution ran into a fracture that coincides perfectly with the colonial fracture.

In the 1960s the problem was clearly formulated by Hans-Jürgen Krahl, a leader of the young Social Democrats and the German student movement: while it is true that there "doesn't exist any example of victorious revolution in the highly developed countries," it is also a fact that revolutions constantly break out in the "third world," which indicates both "the international unity of anticapitalist protest" and "a constellation and a qualitatively new fact: the currentness of revolution. For the first time in the history of capitalism revolution is a generally present and visible possibility, but one that is realized in the oppressed and poor countries of the Third World."

Revolution in the colonies "has no paradigmatic character for the capitalist countries," because in the West, "domination and repression aren't based on material misery and physical oppression." The revolutionary struggles that develop on the two sides of the colonial fracture are not the same and the revolutionary methods that prove victorious in the colonies cannot be transposed to the metropole, where the structure of capital, power, and the exploited subjectivities is not the same.

There remains literally nothing of the global network of parties, organizations, movements, and even states that "worked" towards revolution. The capitalist globalization that destroyed it was a strategic response to world revolution. In spite of that, any politics conceived within the borders of the nation-state is bound to fail.

Civil War or World Revolution?

The "global civil war" of Hannah Arendt, Carl Schmitt, and Rainer Koselleck was actually a series of revolutions. The world revolution, despite its failure after 1917, continued to progress without ever finding an international strategy suited to its objectives. But the "global civil war" can be considered from two points of view: that of the state, biopolitics, the state of exception, fascism, and Nazism (Agamben, Foucault, etc.) and that of "revolution," which is at the origin of all the changes affecting the category of politics and its reality. The revolution revealed that the first point of view was blind to the relation of subordination which the state, biopolitics, states of exception, and the juridical system maintain with capital. There is no autonomy, no operational independence of the political system. The state and biopolitics are no longer anything but centers of implementation of the "decrees" of capital (the governments/governance of the different states during the financial crisis is exemplary in this respect. Capital's machine is a *sui generis* "sovereign" (of which the state now forms part), that makes decisions, chooses, orients itself, and runs the administration, the juidical system, and the police, for its profit and its power.

Politics is in the "economy" (Marx), but provided one understands, along with Lenin, the capitalist relation, not as a mere "social relation," but as a center of strategic confrontation that all the 20th century revolutions subjectified.

Revolution of All Relations of Domination

To the globalization of revolution in the South there corresponded a broadening of struggles that attacked all the capitalist power relations, such that the capital/labor relation was overrun. Capitalism had never seen an offensive combining a global scale of revolutions with a social intensity of struggles. Michel Foucault defined the period 1955–1975 as that of "insurrection of subjugated knowledges." The "effectiveness of the scattered and discontinuous offensives" waged by the subjugated knowledges made possible the "immense and proliferating criticability of things, institutions, discourses"—and the psychiatric institution, "morality" or the "traditional sexual hierarchy," the judicial and penal apparatus, mental illness, the hospital, the school, etc., all came under attack.

To this expansion of struggles there corresponded not an innovation in the theory and practice of revolution, but a fragmentation of viewpoints that were often incompatible, incapable of establishing a strategy against a common enemy. The stuggles that were defeated at the [deletion] end of the 1970s were pregnant with "presents," that is, potentials, which were not actualized but continue to persist (Benjamin). Insofar as they constitute the eternal aspect of every event (Deleuze), these potentials are always virtually "present" and can enter into resonance with actuality through the encounter with a new revolutionary rupture (of which, for the moment, one doesn't see any trace).

The Two Strategies of Revolution

Hans-Jürgen Krahl perfectly sums up the force and the limits of revolution as it has been thought and practiced by the workers' movement.[2] The two principles or strategies of revolution, "socialization" (rules for using violence for the seizure of power, destruction of the state apparatus and expropriation of the expropriators, distribution of the ownership of the means of production) and "communication" (the political struggle for power presupposes that the rules of solidarity already exist in the practice of the organization), which should have been conceived and practiced as inseparable, have proved to be hard to reconcile. "In the past, the workers' movements did not succeed in establishing a relationship between the rules of violence dictated by the struggle for power and the rules of solidarity dictated by the praxis of the organization."

This viewpont is still expressed within the tradition of the workers' movement, whereas Lonzi positions herself outside and Fanon at the boundary. It is not just a question of solidarity (Krahl), or the relationship beween (seizure of) power and communism, as in Benjamin.

Subjugations

With the emergence of movements of women and of the colonized, the contradictions within the revolutionary process seem to break apart and give rise to very different "revolutionary" processes that were practically irreconcilable at the end of the 1960s and that appear even more so today.

The forms of domination and exploitation of women and the colonized are specific and difficult to grasp from the standpoint of the workers' movement, since they add racial and sexual domination to economic exploitation. Overcoming them requires forms of organization and aims of political action very different form those of Leninism.

"The woman is oppressed within the sexual model," Lonzi affirms. What is lacking in socialist theory? she asks. Lenin promised freedom, but didn't accept the process of liberation, which for feminists started with gender. The Marxists succeeded at making a revolution, but the dictatorship of the proletariat proved incapable of "dissolving the social roles." Socialization of the means of production did not weaken the institution of the family, but reinforced it [...] by excluding the woman as an active party in the elaboration of socialist themes."

One can't undo the subjugations of the colonized and of women simply by attacking "production" and the exploitation of labor. The singularities of that fabrication of "subjectivity" ("the woman") demand a political intervention and a form of organization that doesn't just aim at the seizure of power. In the colonial situation, the political work is double, because one cannot "set subjectivity aside." The black revolutionary must wage a dual struggle, "objectively and subjectively." Because "the black soul is a construction of the White," it must be liberated from itself, so that, for Aimé Césaire, "the struggle of the colonial peoples against colonialism, the struggle of peoples of color against racism is much more complex, or rather, of a completely different nature than the struggle of the French worker against French capitalism."

Labor

If the form of the domination of women and the colonized is very different from that of the workers, women's (unpaid) labor is as well.

The manifesto of Rivolta Femminili states that "domestic unpaid labor [is] the service that enables capitalism, private or state, to reproduce itself, while refusing to think of the liberation of women via access to productive labor (Lenin). On the contrary, valorizing "unproductive moments" is an integral part of the life proposed by women. "Productivist competition" is the "power plan" shared by the "societies controlled by private or state capitalism."

In the colonies, the oppositions city/country, workers/lumpen, structure/superstructure cannot function. In that world which European Marxism regards as "premodern" (and therefore ignores), we again encounter a whole series of figures and problems that we are now familiar with. The exploitation of man "assumes different guises" (unemployed, seasonal, lumpen, proletarian, worker, etc) which capital "unifies," not like yesterday, through wage-earning and industry, but, like today, through finance. "Framing the problem of the evolution of underdeveloped countries" by an appeal to productivism, to developmentalism as in the Soviet Union ("Let us gird our loins and set to work"), "appears to us neither right nor reasonable" (Fanon).

What the worker and "labor" have become more resembles the condition of the colonized and women (precarious, unpaid, servile labor) than that of the worker described by Tronti.

Autonomy of the Organization

Women and the colonized call for autonomous organizations to respond to the problems that aren't considered by the theory of the workers' movement.

Perhaps it's in the feminist movement that one finds the most radical critique of the centralization and verticality of power relations in the "party" and the aims of radical organization. The transformation of "social roles," which the revolution postpones to an after-the-revolution, is the immediate object of political practices. In order to become an autonomous political subject, the women invent a radical democracy. Within the self-consciousness groups, they test out new horizontal, non-herarchical relations that would create a collective awareness specific to women. The concept and practice of "representation" and delegation are absent, since the problem is not the seizure, nor the management of power.

Dismantling the roles and the relegation to femininity means not being taken in by the promises of emanicipation *through work* and through *the struggle for power*, which are considered as values of the patriarchal culture (and of the workers' movement). The feminist movement doesn't demand any participation in power, but, quite the opposite, a placing into discussion of the concept of power and seizure of power, because the only thing truly necessary for managing it "is a particular form of alienation."

The feminist movement arrives in this way at separating the practices of the formation and affirmation of the autonomous subject from the question of revolution, by producing two very different and (according to Lonzi) incompatible concepts of politicization.

The Party among the Colonized

The colonized, while practicing a dual struggle, objective (against capitalism) and subjective (against subjugation), introduce other problematizations into the revoloutionary workers' tradition codified by the Bolsheviks.

The party "is a notion imported from the metropole. This instrument of modern struggles is imposed as is" on the protean reality of the colonies. "The party machine appears resistant to any innovation," in the face of a reality that has nothing in common with that described in *Workers and Capital*, because the working class doesn't exist or constitutes a minority.

Not only do the colonized refuse to submit to the hegemony of the working class and the workers' movement, but they call for separate and autonomous modes of organization. The colonial question cannot be treated as part of more important whole, represented by the interests of the Communist Party, Césaire will say.

"The forces fighting colonization can only wither in organizations that are not their own, constructed for them, by them, and designed for ends that only they can determine." Neither the theory nor the consciousness can be brought in from the outside. At the same time as they build their own organizations, the colonized have to work out their own strategies. The critique of representation and delegation also animates them. The peoples don't need a leader, they "aren't herds and they don't need to be led. If the leader is leading me, I want him to know that at the same time I am leading him" (Fanon).

For Fanon, unlike for Lonzi, the "seizure of power" is never in question ("Starting in 1954, the problem which the colonial peoples ponder has been the following: what must be done to create another Dien Bien Phu? [...] the problem had to do with the marshalling of their forces, with their organization, their date of entry into action." The subject and the forms of the revolution were problematized, however. Significantly, *The Wretched of the Earth* submits different answers to the question of the who and how of revolution. Fanon affirms first of all that the revolution can only be global and "will be made with the help of the European masses," even if these have "often rallied, over colonial issues, to the positions of our common masters." Further down, in the conclusions, it's the "third world" which, considering the "sometimes stupendous arguments defended by

Europe," but also "its crimes," has the task of "recommencing a history of man." Here, there is an opposition between "third world" and "Europe" that doesn't seem to take into account what Fanon earlier named "our common masters." The enemy becomes Europe as such; capitalism disappears beneath the racial division. These ambiguities will see an unfortunate reiteration in postcolonial thought, because revolution will be completely vacated.

Critique of the Dialectic

How do we break out of the dialectic and historicism? This is the question that Lonzi and Fanon attempt to answer. While making use of the rich European conceptual arsenal, they deliver a vehement attack on the Hegelian dialectic (and its Marxist translation). The dialectic cannot undo the roles and functions to which women and black people are subjected and by which they are excluded from history and the public sphere. The dialectic's promise of emancipation cannot be kept.

It only concerns conflicts that take place within the "majoritarian model" (man, white, adult, etc.), so that it is "white and male." Blacks and women are "blocked" at "stages" from which they can't advance in order to attain the freedom of self-consciousness.

Forever condemned to their condition of dominated beings, they form the hidden face of globalized capital which Hegel translates into the concepts of the "European spirit."

In the dialectical progression, Fanon will say, one cannot create any meaning, since "it is the meaning that was there, pre-existing, waiting for me." To this historical, predetermined becoming, which already contains its end in itself from its inception, Fanon opposes "unpredictability."

From the point of view of the Marxist dialectic, the struggle depends on the development of the productive forces, following a linearity that Fanon contests. The revolutionary process is a leap, a non-dialectical rupture of the order of history that will open onto the invention and discovery of something that history did not already contain. The unpredictable, as a means of leaving history, is a thematic that one will re-encounter, enriched and broadened, in Lonzi, who clearly spells out, in two ways, the conditions of rupture with the Leninist war machine and the subject that wielded it. First, she declares that the subject is not given, that, quite the opposite, it is "unforeseen," and, second that the temporality of the feminist movement is not the future, but the present. The unforeseen subject implies an "unpredictable act," a rupture creating the possibilities of the subject's own liberation.

Lonzi aims directly at the Marxist revolution, which posits a discontinuity in terms of "power," but a continuity as to the "subject" of the revolution. Revolution (as the subject) is already happening ("the real movement that destroys the present state of things"; it only has to realize itself by taking power, which will enable it to unfold, finally, in forms more rational and more productive than those of capital. In this framework, the temporality of revolution is the future (promise), while the "present" is the temporality of the feminist rupture, the here and now ("*The goal doesn't exist, the present does.*") which starts the process of destruction of the stereotypes of femininity and subjectification.

The 1960s rediscovered the new relation between "present" and revolution that Benjamin made his priority, but having lost the acute awareness he had of the destructive force of capital. While Benjamin is the first, in the Marxist tradition, to theorize revolution as a rupture in the historical continuum from the standpoint of the "present," in the 1960s, there was a blossoming of different theories of the event which tried to conceptualize the "present" that was opened up by the struggles.

This affirmation of history's discontinuity, this critique of its causality and its determinisms, converges with Lonzi's *unforeseen* and Fanon's *unpredictability*: the revolutionary subject derives from, but doesn't depend on, history; if it comes from the economic, political, and social situation, it is not deducible from that situation. It cannot be anticipated by the imagination, by a project, or a program, nor properly grasped by knowledge, science, or theory. What one can know are the conditions it will emerge from, but it isn't possible to anticipate its modes of deployment. Revolution is strictly something "unforeseen," something that one can prepare, organize, promote, but whose subjectification is not contained in the conditions. It is "impossible" in the order of history's causalities, unimaginable on the basis of the economic, social, and political determinisms.

The event comes out of history, breaks with its continuity and, turning aside from its constraints, it creates new possibles, unimaginable and impossible before the rupture, but their actualization is accomplished by falling back into history, by clashing with its "reality." History and the situation from which it bursts forth, but also history and the situation it will fall back into, cannot be defined generically. History and the situation from which the movements of '68 came, and which the event would fall back into are characterized by the "global civil war" and the "world revolution."

Theories of the event underscored the creative moment to the detriment of the destructive moment of political action (although Deleuze warns that one is dealing with a theory for "beautiful souls"), often identified with the Hegelian "negative." What Benjamin still held together under the threat of Nazism is here separated in a theory of "becoming-revolutionary" (reappearing in the aesthetic paradigm of Guattari or in the *parrêsia* of Foucault's last lectures), which seems oblivious of the linkage of "production and destruction" in the revolutionary tradition.

The Workers' Movement

The ambiguities, hesitations, differences, even radical ones, that we have seen unfolding within the world revolution strike against an obstacle that is theoretical and practical at once: the theory and the practice of the workers' movement, which is one of the (major) causes of the defeat.

Tronti represents an innovation inside of Marxism, but without leaving its framework and even exacerbating its limits (at bottom, he may very well represent the viewpoint of the workers' movement, because he's always been a Communist Party man who shares many of its ruts as well as its destiny/decline). In *Workers and Capital*, in order to break out of the dialectic, he rereads the history of the working class by bringing into play the Marxian concepts of the class's *Angriffskraft* (offensive force) and capital's *Widerstandskraft* (defensive force). To the movements of the the working class he ascribes an autonomy and a primacy over those of capital, which would thus find themselves in a defensive, reactive position.

Very soon (two years after publication of the book, 1966), his strategic perspective (against the sociologism and economism of postwar Marxism) is revealed to be largely outmoded by the events of '68, for three basic reasons. The first is the main one: it is completely blind to the rise of the decolonization movements and the feminist movements starting at the end of the 19th century but with a strong acceleration during the First World War and the Soviet Revolution. Defining labor power without the "colonized" and without "women" is a theoretical error even before being a political mistake. It is only a "mutilated" and Eurocentric definition of capitalism, which prevents Tronti from seeing the characteristics of the "world revolution" and its "racial and sexual" extension.

Lenin was never in England, where he was imagined by the title of an article written by Tronti at the beginning of the 1960s. Lenin (or the revolution) made his (its) rounds wherever there was a "delay" in the development of the productive forces, wherever the situation was greatly out of sync with the industrial, scientific, technological center of capitalism, organizing war machines that were not driven mainly by workers but by peasants.

Tronti shows himself to be a less than clear-headed strategist for two other reasons: he asserts the primacy of working-class initiative at the moment it begins to lose all political hegemony and capital is in the process of taking back a political advantage which it will not let go of again. From that moment foreward, the political agenda, the terrain of political confrontation, its form and its content, will always be defined by capital. Tronti failed to grasp that the strength of the class was tied first and foremost to the possibility and the reality of revolution (for Tronti and for the Party, revolution ended with 1917). Without revolution, workers are simply a component of capital. The subsequent attempt to go beyond the "failure" of *operaismo* is based on another strategic error. Tronti declares the autonomy of politics (in reality, the autonomy of the state) at the very moment the state also becomes an element, a component, a cogwheel of the capitalist war machine, without any possible independence remaining.

Faced with the political movements that asserted themselves in the 1970s and with capitalism's recapture of the initiative, Tronti himself recognized the failure of *Workers and Capital*. What would remain of this theory would only be the partisan adoption of the "worker's" point of view.

Only a position that doesn't claim any universality, but a partial viewpoint based on political class interests, can "reconstruct the truth of everything" (of capital). Precisely so, but the fact is that, from the postwar onward, none of the exploited and the dominated identify with the working class; the partisan points of view are numerous and all of them (the feminist movements, the movements of decolonization, the student movements) affirm heterogeneous "truths" and different and often incompatible "everythings." Needless to say, in Tronti and the Party alike, revolution is the remembrance of a European at sunset.[3]

The Exclusion of Revolution in Postcolonial Theory

In the post-'68 movements, the problematizations, the contradictions, the conflicts, the theoretical and political divergences, even radical ones, of the world revolution, quickly turn to depoliticization.

The postcolonial theories, while deepening the critique of the colonial and postcolonial exercise of power, do without the concept and reality of the revolutionary rupture. Here it is appropriate to mention an important author for postcolonial theory, although he denies belonging to it, Achille Mbembe. Mbembe deploys and broadens the concept of thanato-politics, barely sketched out by

Foucault, constructing its genealogy on the basis of the black slave trade (necropolitics), and yet he excludes the horizon of revolution. "The hope for a new victory over the Master is no longer the thing. We've stopped waiting for the Master's death. We no longer believe he is mortal. The Master no longer being mortal, we're left with one illusion, namely, partaking in the Master's world."[4] Obviously, this statement gives rise to multiple interpretations—but the turnaround he suggests, and even his conception of a "becoming-black of the world," as interesting as it is, leaves any revolutionary rupture entirely aside.

As for the theoreticians of postcolonial studies, they claim to be both the radical thinkers of our time and the heirs of the struggles for national liberation and the anti-imperialist revolutions (their starting point is in their inquiry as to the reasons for the failure of revolutions, but they never consider the new conditions that may give rise to them, as if the defeat had put a permanent end to their possibility). Without going into the complexity and the differences of positions, one thing doesn't cease to amaze: their point of view has nothing to do with that of the colonized of the 19th century whose lineage they claim. Their critique of Europe, of Eurocentrism, of the categories devised by European thought, etc. is far removed from the way in which the colonized and the slaves related to the "center" of the capitalism of their epoch.

The colonized easily understood what the postcolonial theoreticians don't manage to see. Europe is assuredly the home of colonial conquest, the origin of the absolute violence brought to bear on the colonial populations, but it is also the place where revolution was invented. The French Revolution carried with it a "bourgeois" determination to maintain slavery, subordinate women, and subjugate the propertyless, but neither the slaves of Saint-Domingue, nor Olympe de Gouges with her Declaration of the Rights of the Woman, nor the sans-culottes missed the opportunity to revolt, even to make a true revolution (Haiti) while laying the foundations for the struggles to come. When the revolution became proletarian and Europe began to produce anti-capitalist theories (Marxism in particular) and "revolutionary" forms of organization, the semi-colonized and the colonized didn't ask themselves whether the categories of power and subjectivity created in Europe corresponded to their reality: they put them to use. It was a revolutionary with slanting eyes who made, with theoretical tools forged in Europe and adapted to the Russian situation, the first victorious proletarian revolution, opening the door to revolution not in the West, but in the East and later in the world's South.

The colonized, very selective, took from Europe what suited them best, the critique of capitalism, a mode of global domination which, obviously, was articulated differently in the West and in the East. Shifting towards the east then spreading into the South, the revolution transformed itself, critiquing Marxist historicism, breaking with its theory of stages, reconfiguring the theory of the revolutionary subject through the involvement of the peasantry, revising the theory of the party (Fanon), of class (Cabral), the relationship between structure and superstructure, "distending Marxism," inventing a new function for "culture," etc., but always staying faithful to the project of superseding capitalism.

The failure of world revolution resulted from the inability to establish a subjective strategy capable of actualizing it by integrating all these transformations and these critiques. The revolution soon fell back on "socialism in one country" and on the different nationalisms, while the Western working class and its institutions, blind to the new political subjects in the process of affirmation, incorporated the logic of capital.

If the question of how to "provincialize Europe" is a strategic inquiry for these theories, the problem has no longer been on the table for some time, seeing that Europe has taken care of that since the First World War, and doubly so, by losing its ability to be the center of capitalism and the arena of revolution. The postcolonial point of view is that of dominated individuals confined within domination, whereas the colonized of the 20th century, starting from their "enslavement," affirmed revolution. The positioning is very different: the first are led in a more or less radical way to the posture of "victim," the second, to revolutionary subjectification.

Reconnecting with Revolution

The division between constitution of the subject and revolution, which finds its most coherent presentation in the texts of Lonzi, could be conceptualized and generalized with the categories of Gilles Deleuze. To counter the attacks undergone by "revolution" after its politico-military defeat of the 1960s, he distinguishes "revolutions" (which always end badly!) from the "becoming-revolutionary" of participants in the revolutionary process. This becoming-revolutionary continues beyond the failure of the revolutions themselves. Many of the post-'68 movements seem to have built their strategy on this separation of the "becoming-revolutionary" (critique of the subjugations, differential production of subjectivity, autonomy and independence of the "forms of life," affirmation and care of "self") and "revolution" (radical change of the property regime, struggle for political power, expropriation of the expropriators, supersession of capitalism). This separation corresponds to the distinction between emancipation and revolution, in which the first consists of the escape of all sorts of minorities (sexual, racial, ethnic) from their state of inferiority, exclusion, and domination in which capitalism has confined them, whereas the second requires the exit from capitalism. The abolition of slavery had demonstrated the limits of a politics based solely on emancipation, which did not prevent the transition from one racial segregation to another. The "creative" dimension of political action is thus separated radically from the "destructive" dimension.

But is it possible to break the close relation that links revolution to the becoming-revolutionary? Can the process of production and differentiation of subjectivity take place without aiming, simultaneously, for the demise of capitalism and the state? Forty years of neoliberal domination seem to have shown that without a relation and a mutual enrichment of revolution and the becoming-revolutionary, both grow inexorably weaker.

The strategy of autonomization of the "becoming-revolutionary" is pursued and developed not only by most of the feminist and queer movements, but also by the expressions of critical thinking born out of the struggles of the 1960s in the West. The constitution of a revolutionary subject without a revolution is also found in Negri, for whom the cognitive worker becomes "more and more autonomous and independent" as production defined as biopolitical develops. Cognitive workers acquire a power that is strictly tied to their function in production, prior to any revolutionary organization and practice, since the work of the "cognitariat" is formative of the world and its relations (ontological labor). The force of autonomy and independence which this collective worker accumulates in and against biopolitical production constitutes an "exodus" in action, a process of exit from capitalism that is already underway. Revolution may only serve to affirm what is already there (the commons of teamwork). Jacques Rancière further accentuates this dissociation between revolution and becoming-revolutionary, by affirming the existence of two types of conflict, the conflict of forces (class struggle and the Marxist tradition) and the conflict of worlds (the subjective self-affirmation of the political subject's autonomy): revolution/emancipation. Political action as the invention of names that shatter social identification, that explode the mediations of the consensual order by deploying an autonomous time which creates new forms of life doesn't set forces, but worlds, in opposition. The newness of '68 would reside in the dissociation it brought about between a conflict of worlds and conflicts of forces.

This dissociation plays dirty tricks, because the world of equality of political movements and that of capitalist inequality don't proceed in parallel fashion. The world of inequality, indissociable from the exercise of force, has systematically undone the world of equality, reducing the spaces of "secession" almost to nothing. Inequality crosses another threshold with the application of force by the new fascisms.

We cannot push our reflections further because, as Krahl explained it, a "revolutionary theory" is not the same thing as a "theory of revolution." A revolutionary theory (all, or nearly all, of '68 thought) represents society in terms of its possible transformation by exposing relations of domination, whereas a theory of revolution indicates specific strategic principles: this is the task that falls to a revolutionary organization and to future revolutionaries.

Notes

Introduction: Apocalyptic Times

1. Wendy Brown, "Le néoliberalisme sape la démocracie," *AOC*, January 5, 2019. Online: aoc.media/entretien/2019/01/05/wendy-brown-néoliberalisme-sape-democratie2.

2. Alain Duhamel, "Le triomphe de la haine en politique," *Libération*, January 9, 2019.

3. Samuel Hayat thus explains, regarding the Yellow Vests: "We are dealing with a revolutionary movement, but one without revolution in the narrowly political sense: it's a social revolution, at least in process" (Samuel Hayat, "Liberation movements have to adapt to circumstances," *Ballast*, February 20, 2019, Online: www.revue-ballast.fr/samuel-hayat-les-mouvements-demanicipation).

1. When Capital Goes to War

1. Michael Goebel, *Paris, capitale du tiers-monde. Comment est née la révolution anticoloniale (1919–1939)*, trans. P. Stockman, Paris, La découverte, 2017.

2. Eliane Brum, "Brésil: comment résister en ces temps de brutalité," *La Règle du jeu*, October 17, 2018. Online: laregledujeu.org/ 2018/ 10/17/34436/bresil-comment-resister-en-ces-temps-de-brutalite.

3. The analysis that follows draws on the remarkable work by Lena Lavinas, *The Takeover of Social Policy by Financialization: The Brazilian Paradox*, New York, Palgrave MacMillan, 2016; see also Lena Lavinas, "How Social Developmentalism Reframed Social Policy in Brazil," *New Political Economy*, vol. 22, #6, 2017.

4. For an in-depth analysis of debt, see my books *The Making of the Indebted Man* (South Pasadena, CA, Semiotext(e)) and *Governing by Debt* (South Pasadena, CA, Semiotext(e), 2015).

5. Michel Crozier, Samuel Huntington, and Joji Watanuki, *The Crisis of Democracy: On the Governability of Democracies*, New York, New York University Press, 1975.

6. Perry Anderson, "Crisis in Brazil," *London Review of Books*, April 2016.

7. For example, the alliance coming out of the Italian elections of 2018 between the (populist) Five Star Movement and the (fascist) League demonstrates all the political inconsistency of populism. It enabled the neo-fascists not only to enter the government but to become, in a few months, the number one Italian party. It was enough for Salvini, Minister of the Interior and member of the League, to pronounce the magic words "the gates are closed" (to migrants) to blank out all the wishful thinking expressed by the Five Star Movement. Populism (including left populism) opens up and prepares the new fascisms' access to power.

8. Michel Foucault, "La philosophie analytique et la politique" (1978), *Dits et écrits*, vol. II, Paris, Gallimard, 2001, p. 536.

9. Adam Tooze, "Quand les américains aimaient Mussolini," *Esprit*, May 2017.

10. *Ibid.*, p. 68–69.

11. Jean-Paul Sartre, "Colonialisme et néo-colonialisme." *Situations*, VI, Paris, Gallimard, 1964, p. 54.

12. Frantz Fanon, *Les Damnés de la terre* (1961), *Oeuvres*, Paris, La Découverte, 2011, p. 509.

13. Guy Burgel, "Les fins de mois difficiles avant la fin du monde," *Libération*, November 26, 2018.

14. Jean-Paul Sartre, *Réflections sur la question juive* (1946), Paris, Gallimard, p. 29.

15. *Ibid.*, p. 62

16. In this connection, the book by Deborah Cowen, *The Deadly Life of Logistics: Mapping Violence in Global Trade* (Minneapolis,

University of Minnesota Press, 2014), is exemplary (all the quotations concerning logistics are excerpted from it). This work was brought to my attention by Carlotta Benvegnu.

17. Sankara would be murdered only five months after this talk. The other powerful apparatus of monetary neocolonialism in Africa, the CFA franc, through which France continues to keep the economies of fourteen African countries (plus the Comoros Islands) under its yoke, was also denounced by Sankara: "The CFA franc, tied to the French monetary system, is a weapon of French domination. The capitalist merchant bourgeoisie built its fortune on the backs of our people with the help of this connection, this monetary monopoly."

18. Michel Foucault, *Sécurité, territoire, population. Cours au Collège de France, 1977–1978*, Paris, Gallimard/Le Seuil, p. 46, p. 67.

19. Silvia Federici, *Reincantare il mondo*, Verona, Ombre Corte, p. 62 [*Re-enchanting the World*, Oakland, CA: PM Press, p. 40].

20. *Ibid.*, p. 59. [cf. pp. 37–38, English edition].

21. *Ibid.*

22. *Ibid.* p. 90–91.

23. For an extensive treatment of this, see the book I wrote with Éric Alliez, *Guerres et Capital*, Paris, Amsterdam, 2016. [*Wars and Capital*, South Pasadena, CA, Semiotext(e), 2018]

24. Fabio Mini, *La Guerra spiegata a…*, Turin, Einaudi, 2013.

25. *Ibid.*, p. 74.

26. *Ibid.*, p. 39.

27. Thierry Voeltzel, *Vingt ans et après*, Paris, Verticales, 2014, p. 150.

28. Inexplicably, when Foucault develops the relationship between biopolitics and Nazism, he doesn't deal with the most important event of the first half of the 20th century, 1917. "The impact of the Soviet revolution marked Germany like no other country. The political dividing line that traversed the history of the following decades crystallized the hopes, hatreds, and fears of a population

split in two, during a confrontation that was historic" (Donatella di Cesare, *Heidegger, les Juifs, la Shoah. Les Cahiers noirs*, French trans. G. Deniau, Paris, Le Seuil, 2016, p. 222).

29. Fabio Mini, *La Guerra spiegata a…*, *op. cit.*, p. 35.

30. Walter Benjamin, "Critique de la violence," *Oeuvres*, Paris, Gallimard, 2000, p. 224 [*Selected Writings*, Vol. 1, Cambridge, Mass., Harvard University Press, 1996, p. 243].

31. Michel Foucault, *Le Pouvoir psychiatrique. Cours au Collège de France, 1973–1974*, Paris, Gallimard/Le Seuil, 2003, p. 53.

32. Michel Foucault, *Sécurité, territoire, population*, *op. cit.* p. 22.

33. Michel Foucault, *Naissance de la Biopolitique. Cours au Collège de France, 1978–1979*, Paris, Gallimard/Le Seuil, 2004, p. 261.

34. Félix Guattari, *Lignes de fuite*, La Tour d'Aigues, L'Aube, 2011, p. 54.

35. Michael Hardt and Antonio Negri, *Commonwealth*, French trans. E. Boyer, Paris, Stock, 2012. [*Commonwealth*, Cambridge, Mass, Harvard University Press, 2009.]

36. *Ibid.*, p. 29. [Eng. edition, p. 7.]

37. Patrice Spinosi, an attorney at the Council of State and the Cour de Cassation, quoted by Ellen Salvi, "Cette loi 'anticasseurs' ne menace pas le délinquant, elle menace le citoyen" ["This 'anti-riot' law doesn't threaten the delinquent, it threatens the citizen"], *Mediapart*, February 3, 2019.

38. He adds: "A fundamental freedom has disappeared. There wouldn't be any reason, moreover, not to expand this fine system, and it will come to that some day, no doubt. The dikes have given way. Anything is possible now […] I don't know where 'progressivism' is in this majority or in this government, but it is certainly not in the domain of public freedoms. They are venturing things straight out of the repressive 19th century. It is truly stupefying that no one sees the political contradiction between the asserted fight against 'populism' and this kind of legislation" (François Sureau, "C'est le citoyen qu'on intimide, et pas le délinquant" ["It's the citizen

who's being intimidated, and not the delinquent"], *Le Monde*, February 4, 2019).

39. What must be examined is not "the immediate unity of politics and life," but the unity that capital would like to establish with life. In capitalism, life is not like "bare life" divided into its forms, but life delivered over to the forces that constitute it. What it must absolutely be separated from is its political form (revolution), under penalty of physical destruction. This theory reproduces a misconception that one already finds in Foucault. The problem is not the biological, but the (anorganic) potentiality of forces. In Marx, the force of labor is one of those "living" forces that cannot be defined by biology and require something other than "political theology" in order for tasks to be imposed on it and for its powers to be harnessed.

40. Franz Fanon, *Les Damnés de la terre, Oeuvres, op. cit.*, p. 485.

41. Michel Foucault, *"Il faut défendre la société," Cours au college de France, 1976*, Paris, Gallimard/Le Seuil, 1996, p. 194.

42. "It would be reductive to consider Nazi antisémitisme as simply 'biological.' Under the cloak of science, or pseudo-science, ancient theological prejudices resurfaced […]. Hitlerian antisemitism is a political and theological union between racism and apocalypse" (Donatella di Cesare, *Heidegger, les Juifs, la Shoah, op. cit.* p. 148). She adds: "Contrary to what is believed, the Nuremberg Laws are not based on 'scientific' criteria; it was only for propaganda purposes that they were termed 'racial laws,' since the racist inventions never found any empirical justification, which made the recourse to theology necessary" (*ibid.*, p. 160).

43. Michel Foucault, "La philosophie analytique et la politique" (1978), *Dits et Écrits*, vol. II, *op.cit.*, p. 545.

44. Michel Foucault, *"Il faut défendre la société," op. cit.*, p. 187.

45. Michel Foucault, *Histoire de la sexualité I: La Volonté de savoir*, Paris, Gallimard, 1976, p. 167.

46. Gilles Deleuze, *L'Île déserte et autres textes*, Paris, Minuit, 2002, p. 366.

47. Walter Benjamin, *Rue à sens unique* ["One-Way Street"], Paris, Allia, 2015, p. 74.

48. Michel Foucault, "Méthodologie pour la connaissance du monde: comment se débarraser du marxisme" (1978), *Dits et Écrits II, op. cit.*, p. 605.

49. Michel Foucault, *Histoire de la sexualité*, vol. I, *op. cit.*, p. 124.

50. *Ibid.* p. 123.

51. *Ibid.*, p. 131.

52. The concepts of "labor," "production," and "class" would benefit greatly from being understood in terms of strategic relations. The post-operaist position, ontologizing work and workers, attributes a primacy to (cognitive) workers' activity that is nowhere to be found. Political initiative is not contained in an ontology of the human being's productivity, but in that being's capacity to affirm its own political strength through a negation, a rupture. The ontology of labor makes the world appear upside down: the multitude sets the political agenda and capital painfully follows, capturing its productivity.

53. Michel Foucault, *Histoire de la sexualité*, vol I, *op. cit.*, p. 123.

54. Teresa de Lauretis, "La gaia scienza, ovvero la Traviata Norma," in Mario Mieli, *Elementi di critique omosessuale*, Milan, Feltrinelli, 2017, p. 266.

55. Claude Rabant writes this about Mario Mieli, author of the most important theoretical essay of the homosexual liberation movement in Italy: "As Mieli has repeated several times, it is a war. The conflict is not just intra-discursive, aimed at legitimating an experience, it is also real and extra-discursive—that is, hand-to-hand [...]. This critique is a conquest of territory, the new appropriation of a territory that is the equivalent of a self-appropriation. He is talking about a war that unavoidably attacks the territory of the dominant other, that causes problems for that other, not just locally but globally" (Claude Rabant, "Un clamore sospeso tra la vita e la morte," in Mario Mieli, *Elementi di critique omosessuale*, *op, cit.*, p. 292).

2. Technical Machine and War Machine

1. Catherine Malabou, *Métamorphoses de l'intelligence. Que faire de leur cerveau bleu?*, Paris, PUF, 2017, p. 124.

2. Lewis Mumford, *Le Mythe de la machine*, 2 vol. (1967 and 1970), Paris, Fayard, 1974. [*The Myth of the Machine*, New York, Harcourt, Brace and World, 1967]

3. *Ibid.*, vol. I, p. 262. [Eng. edition, p. 196]

4. *Ibid.*, p. 256. [Eng. p. 192]

5. *Ibid.*, p.264. [Eng. p. 198]

6. *Ibid.*, p. 263. [Eng p. 197]

7. *Ibid.*, p. 265. [Eng. p.199]

8. Günther Anders, *Nous, fils d'Eichmann*, fr. trans. P. Ivernel, Paris: Rivages, 1988, p. 92–93.

9. "Order," "threat," and insult already characterized communication in the colonies, as will be noted in the next section with Fanon.

10. Franz Fanon, *L'An V de la revolution algérienne*, *Oeuvres*, Paris, La Découverte, 2011, p. 303–330, (all the quotes that follow are drawn from this chapter) [*A Dying Colonialism*, New York, Grove Press, 1994, p. 69–97]

11. Peter Galison, "The Ontology of the Enemy and the Cybernetic Vision," *Critical Inquiry*, vol. 21, no 1, 1994. "Black box" is an expression that dates from the Second World War, from the period of the research focused on radar, and means that the circuits internal to the "box" function without anyone needing to understand how the circuit was put in place.

12. Franco Piperno, "Il 68. sociale, politico, culturale," *Alafabeta materiali*, Rome, DeriveApprodi, 2018.

13. Fred Turner, *Aux sources de l'utopie numérique. De la contre-culture à la cyberculture*, Fr. trans. L. Vannini, Caen, C&F, 2012.

14. *Ibid.*, p. 369.

15. *Ibid.*, p. 58.

16. Norbert Wiener, *Cybernétique et société*, 1952, Paris, Le Seuil. 2014.

17. *Ibid.*

18. *Ibid.*, p. 185.

19. *Ibid.*, p. 186.

20. Jean-François Lyotard, *Misère de la philosophie*, Paris, Galilée, 2000, p. 114.

21. Jean-François Lyotard, *Moralités postmodernes*, Paris, Galiliée, 1993, p. 68.

22. Gilbert Simondon, *Du mode d'existence des objets techniques* (1958), Paris, Aubier, 2012, p. 175.

23. *Ibid.*, p. 332.

24. Gilles Deleuze and Félix Guattari, *L'Anti-Oedipe. Capitalisme et schizophrénie*, Paris, Minuit, 1972, p. 481.

25. Gilbert Simondon, *Du mode d'existence des objets techniques*, *op.cit.*, p. 174.

26. Gilbert Simondon, *L'Individuation psychique et collective*, Paris, Aubier, 1989, p. 278.

27. Gilles Deleuze and Félix Guattari, *L'Anti-Oedipe, op. cit.*, p. 276.

28. *Ibid.*, p. 277.

29. *Ibid*, p. 278.

30. *Du mode d'existence des objets techniques, op.cit.*, p. 175.

31. Félix Guattari, *Chaosmose*, Paris, Galilée, p. 54.

32. Gilbert Simondon, *L'Individuation psychique et collective, op. cit.*, p. 271.

33. *Ibid.*, p. 272.

34. *Ibid.*, p. 274–275.

35. *Ibid.*, p. 274.

36. Catherine Malabou, *Métamorphoses de l'intelligence, op. cit.*, p. 152.

37. Gilbert Simondon, *Du mode d'existence des objets techniques, op. cit.*, p. 363.

38. Grégoire Chamayou, *Théorie du drone*, Paris, La Fabrique, 2013, p. 287.

39. *Ibid.*, p. 299.

40. *Ibid.* p. 299–301.

41. *Ibid.*, p. 304.

42. Marie-Anne Dujarier, *Le Management desincarné. Enquête sur les nouveaux cadres du travail*, Paris, La Découverte, 2015. All the quotes that follow are from this book.

43. In weakly capitalized enterprises (schools, law courts, etc.) the management program serves as constant capital, since it is what decides ways of doing, times of implementation, rythms of activity, quality of production, etc. Wheareas in a factory many of these prescriptions are incorporated into the operation of the machines (many, because the power incorporated in the machine is doubled by the power of the social machine which also involves its exercise directly on persons). Software and hardware constitute a new type of "constant capital" that can be called "social," since it is a universal machine that goes well with any kind of activity. This type of constant capital requires enormous investments, while it consumes 8% of the world's energy.

44. "What it wants to sell is services, and what it wants to buy is shares. It is no longer a capitalism for production, but for the product—that is, for selling or for the market" (Gilles Deleuze, "Post-scriptum sur les sociétés de contrôle," *Pourparlers*, Paris, Minuit, 2003, p. 245).

45. Walter Benjamin, "Edward Fuchs, collectioneur et historien," Fr. trans. R. Rochlitz, *Oeuvres*, Paris, Gallimard, 2000, p. 181–182. ["Edward Fuchs, Collector and Historian," trans. M.

Jennings and H. Eiland, *Selected Writings*, vol 3., Cambridge, Mass., Harvard U. Press, 2002, p. 265.]

46. The employers dream in fact of "a new capitalism" in which the savings of wage-earners and the population, the pension funds, medical insurance, etc., "being managed in a competitive universe, would again become a function of the enterprise." In 1999, Denis Kessler (the Medef number two) estimated at 2,600 billion francs (150% of the state budget) the booty which the social expenditures would represent for the service enterprises. Privatization of the social security mechanisms, the individualization of social policy, and the determination to make social protection a function of the enterprise are at the heart of the plan to destroy the "European model."

47. Günther Anders, *L'Obsolescence de l'homme. Sur l'âme à l'époque de la deuxième révolution industrielle*, Fr. trans. C. David, Paris. L'Encyclopédie des nuisances, 2002, p. 320.

48. *Ibid.*, p. 322.

49. *Ibid.*, p. 325.

50. Cf. Michael Hardt and Antonio Negri, *Commonwealth*, Fr. trans. E. Boyer, Paris, Stock, 2012, especially the fifth part and more precisely the paragraph titled "The One Divides in Two."

51. Post-workerism doesn't see that what it regards as an inability to integrate is a political choice of separation on the part of capital, a quite real separation, as we have already noted above, at the level of the enterprise as well as at a more general level. Labor capacity will not be integrated into capital, but not because of its power: because of its immense weakness! Non-integration signifies not "autonomy" and "independence," but servile labor.

52. This "productivist" point of view is carried to its extreme consequences by Roberto Ciccarelli (*Forza lavoro. Il lato oscuro della revoluzione digitale*, Rome. DeriveApprodi, 2018), which makes labor power the expression of "being's productivity." Giso Amendola offers this comment about it: "Just as the Spinozian substance is the immanent cause of the infinite modes that express it but do not exhaust it, labor power is always entirely present in

its productive effort, a conatus that is never exhausted and 'defined' by its particular products" ("Il motore invisible. Virtualità e potenza della 'forza lavoro,'" *Opera viva*, February 26, 2018. Online: https://operavivamagazine.org/il-motore-invisible). The conflict comes after, and obviously, it has a hard time coming. Be that as it may, it's the "blockage of productivity" that would give rise to the conflict.

3. Becoming-Revolutionary and Revolution

1. The book, *Guerres et Capital* [*Wars and Capital*], written with Éric Alliez, was conceived as the first part of a project whose second part will deal with the concept and reality of revolution. I present here some of the hypotheses that run through the book that we are writing.

2. Rancière reproduces, fifty years later, the same judgment without advancing a single step: "All of modern history has been traversed by the tension between a class struggle conceived as the formation of an army for defeating the enemy and a class struggle thought of as the secession of a people inventing its institutions and its autonomous forms of life."

3. But the first prize for blindness goes to Althusser: "It's enough to see how the Party was able to digest the events of May, integrate them into its traditional line, how in particular it was able to treat the student movement, to see that is quite capable of *absorbing* even a massive movement, and to maintain its leadership of it. The current policy, which consists in foregrounding the CGT and in continuing to subsist in its shadow—this clever and effective division of labor proves that the Party possesses a large margin of maneuver, in which mechanisms preventive of action assure it a maximum of security" (Louis Althusser, *Écrits sur l'histoire*, Paris, Puf, 2018, p. 88).

4. Achille Mbembe, *Politiques de l'inimitié*, Paris, La Découverte, 2016, p. 169.

ABOUT THE AUTHOR

Maurizio Lazzarato is a sociologist and philosopher in Paris. He is the author of *Governing by Debt* and *Signs and Machines: Capitalism and the Production of Subjectivity*, both published by Semiotext(e).